David Seda~~...~~ *Naked*, *Holidays on Ice*, *Me Talk Pretty One Day*, *Dress Your Family in Corduroy and Denim*, *When You Are Engulfed in Flames*, *Squirrel Seeks Chipmunk*, *Let's Explore Diabetes with Owls* and *Theft by Finding*. He is a regular contributor to the *New Yorker* and BBC Radio 4. He lives in England.

'Unquestionably the king of comic writing ... *Calypso* is both funnier and more heartbreaking than pretty much anything out there' Hadley Freeman, *Guardian*

'We get more of a glimpse than we have before of what lies behind the carapace of a writer who seems able to turn almost any situation to comic gold ... [an] incredibly funny and sometimes moving meditation on love, death and family life, by a master of his craft' *Sunday Times*

'Entrancing ... This book allows us to observe not just the nimble-mouthed elf of his previous work, but a man in his seventh decade expunging his darker secrets and contemplating mortality ... The brilliance of David Sedaris's writing is that his very essence, his aura, seeps through the pages of his books like an intoxicating cloud, mesmerising us so that his logic becomes ours' Alan Cumming, *New York Times*

'*Calypso* is another triumph from the dinner-table raconteur we all wish we could be, a writer whose lightness of touch makes you confront the hardest of truths – and laugh out loud' *Esquire*

'Hilarious and moving ... Sedaris may well be the master of the deadpan delivery – there's plenty of laughing out loud while you read. But *Calypso* is also a tender portrait of a family, flawed – like any other – but doing their best to love each other' Lucy Scholes, *Independent*

'This is a darker, deeper David Sedaris writing about his sister's suicide, the inevitability of ageing and how it's impossible to take a vacation away from yourself, but, rest assured, he's still one of the funniest, most perceptive writers alive' *Red*

'Although Sedaris is famous for being funny, he does pain heartbreakingly well. His observations are wry and witty and eye-wateringly honest and you'll be so sad when it's over' *Evening Standard*

'First-rate comedy gold ... For Sedaris, the boundary between light and dark is blurred. Life's pain and humiliation coexist in every living moment with its jollity and deliciousness. Which elevates his musings on the bodily and social travails of being a man in late middle age to a level of seriously sublime silliness. As ever, Sedaris's irreverent writing is a serious joy; this collection is a must for anyone with a strong stomach who needs a laugh' Melissa Katsoulis, *The Times*

'Heartbreak and hilarity collide ... [*Calypso*] captures the surrealism of the mundane and the funny old thing we like to call life' *Attitude*

Also by David Sedaris

Theft by Finding
Let's Explore Diabetes with Owls
Squirrel Seeks Chipmunk
When You Are Engulfed in Flames
Dress Your Family in Corduroy and Denim
Me Talk Pretty One Day
Holidays on Ice
Naked
Barrel Fever

Calypso

David Sedaris

ABACUS

ABACUS

First published in the United States in 2018 by Little, Brown and Company
First published in Great Britain in 2018 by Little, Brown
This paperback edition published in 2019 by Abacus

12

Acknowledgement is made to the following, in which the stories in this
collection first appeared, some differently titled or in slightly different form:
The New Yorker: "Company Man," "Now We Are Five," "Stepping Out,"
"The Perfect Fit," "Leviathan," "A Modest Proposal," "Untamed,"
"Why Aren't You Laughing?"; *The Guardian:* "Calypso,"
"The One(s) Who Got Away"; *The Paris Review:*
"A Number of Reasons I've Been Depressed Lately," "The Spirit World";
Condé Nast Traveller (UK): "Your English Is So Good."

A CIP catalogue record for this book
is available from the British Library.

ISBN 978-0-349-14189-3

Printed and bound in Great Britain by
Clays Ltd, Elcograf S.p.A.

Papers used by Abacus are from well-managed forests
and other responsible sources.

Abacus
An imprint of
Little, Brown Book Group
Carmelite House
50 Victoria Embankment
London EC4Y 0DZ

An Hachette UK Company
www.hachette.co.uk

www.littlebrown.co.uk

For Joan Lacey

Contents

Company Man

Though there's an industry built on telling you otherwise, there are few real joys to middle age. The only perk I can see is that, with luck, you'll acquire a guest room. Some people get one by default when their kids leave home, and others, like me, eventually trade up and land a bigger house. "Follow me," I now say. The room I lead our visitors to has not been hastily rearranged to accommodate them. It does not double as an office or weaving nook but exists for only one purpose. I have furnished it with a bed rather than a fold-out sofa, and against one wall, just like in a hotel, I've placed a luggage rack. The best feature, though, is its private bathroom.

"If you prefer a shower to a tub, I can put you upstairs in the *second* guest room," I say. "There's a luggage rack up there as well." I hear these words coming from my puppet-lined mouth and shiver with middle-aged satisfaction. Yes, my hair is gray and thinning. Yes, the washer on my penis has worn out, leaving me to dribble urine long after I've zipped my trousers back up. But I have two guest rooms.

The consequence is that if you live in Europe, they attract guests—lots of them. People spend a fortune on their plane tickets from the United States. By the time they arrive they're broke and tired and would probably sleep in our car if we offered it. In Normandy, where we used to have a country place, any visitors were put up in the attic, which doubled as Hugh's studio and smelled of oil paint and decaying mice. It had a rustic cathedral ceiling but no heat, meaning it was usually either too cold or too hot. That house had only one bathroom, wedged between the kitchen and our bedroom. Guests were denied the privacy a person sometimes needs on the toilet, so twice a day I'd take Hugh to the front door and shout behind us, as if this were normal behavior, "We're going out for exactly twenty minutes. Does anyone need anything from the side of the road?"

That was another problem with Normandy: there was nothing for our company to do except sit around. Our village had no businesses in it and the walk to the nearest village that did was not terribly pleasant. This is not to say that our visitors didn't enjoy themselves—just that it took a certain kind of person, outdoorsy and self-motivating. In West Sussex, where we currently live, having company is a bit easier. Within a ten-mile radius of our house, there's a quaint little town with a castle in it and an equally charming one with thirty-seven antique stores. There are chalk-speckled hills one can hike up, and bike trails. It's a fifteen-minute drive to the beach and an easy walk to the nearest pub.

Guests usually take the train from London, and before we pick them up at the station I remind Hugh that, for the duration of their visit, he and I will be playing the role of a perfect couple. This means no bickering and no contradicting each other. If I am seated at the kitchen table and he is standing behind me, he is to place a hand on my shoulder, right on the spot where a parrot would perch if I were a pirate instead of the ideal boyfriend. When I tell a story he has heard so often he could lip-synch it, he is to pretend to be hearing it for the first time and to be appreciating it as much as or more than our guests are. I'm to do the same, and to feign delight when he serves something I hate, like fish with little bones in it. I really blew this a few years back when his friend Sue came for the night and he poached what might as well have been a hairbrush. Blew it to such an extent that after she left I considered having her killed. "She knows too much," I said to Hugh. "The woman's a liability now and we need to contain her."

His friend Jane saw some ugliness as well, and though I like both her and Sue and have known them for going on twenty years, they fall under the category of "Hugh's guests." This means that though I play my role, it is not my responsibility to entertain them. Yes, I offer the occasional drink. I show up for meals but can otherwise come and go at my leisure, exiting, sometimes, as someone is in the middle of a sentence. My father has done this all his life. You'll be talking to him and he'll walk away—not angry but just sort of finished with you. I was probably six years old the first time I noticed this. You'd think I'd have found it hurtful, but instead I looked at his retreating back, thinking, *We can get away with that? Really? Yippee!*

Three of my sisters visited us in Sussex the Christmas of 2012, so Gretchen and Amy took a guest room each. Hugh and I gave Lisa the master bedroom and moved next door to the converted stable I use as my office. One of the things he noted during their stay was that, with the exception of Amy and me, no one in my family ever says goodnight. Rather, they just leave the room—sometimes halfway through dinner—and reappear the following morning. My sisters were considered my guests, but because there was a group of them and they could easily entertain one another, I was more or less free to go about my business. Not that I didn't spend time with them. In various pairings we went on walks and bike rides, but otherwise they sat in the living room talking, or gathered in the kitchen to study Hugh at the stove. I'd join them for a while and then explain that I had some work to do. This meant going next door to the stable, where I'd switch on my computer and turn to Google, thinking, *I wonder what Russell Crowe is up to.*

One of the reasons I'd invited these three over—had gone so far as to buy their tickets—was that this felt like a last hurrah. Except for Paul, who has no passport but tells me with great certainty that, according to an electrician he met on a job site, it is possible to buy one at the airport, we are all in our fifties now. Healthwise, we've been fortunate, but it's just a matter of time before our luck runs out and one of us gets cancer. Then we'll be picked off like figures at a shooting gallery, easy targets given the lives we've led.

I'd counted the days until my sisters' arrival, so why wasn't I next door, sitting with Hugh in our perfect-couple sixteenth-century kitchen with its stone floor and crackling fire? Perhaps I worried that if I didn't wander off, my family would get on my nerves, or—far more likely—I would get on theirs, and that our week together wouldn't be as ideal as I'd told myself it would be. As it was, I'd retreat to my office and spend some time doing nothing of consequence. Then I'd head back into the house and hear something that made me wish I'd never left. It was like walking into a theater an hour after the picture has started, thinking, *How did that kangaroo get his hands on those nunchakus?*

One of the stories I entered late concerned some pills my sister Gretchen had started taking a year and a half earlier. She didn't say what they were prescribed for, but they were causing her to walk and eat in her sleep. I saw this happen the previous Thanksgiving, which we spent together in a rental house in Hawaii. Dinner was served at seven o'clock, and around midnight, an hour or so after she'd gone to bed, Gretchen drifted out of her room. Hugh and I looked up from our books and watched her enter the kitchen. There, she took the turkey out of the refrigerator and started twisting off meat with her fingers. "Why don't you get a plate?" I asked, and she looked at me, not scornfully but blankly, as if it had been the wind talking. Then she reached into the carcass and yanked out some stuffing. This was picked at selectively, one crouton mysteriously favored over another, until she decided she'd had enough, at which point she returned to her room, leaving the mess behind her.

"What was that about?" I asked her the next morning.

Gretchen's face adjusted itself for bad news. "What was what about?"

I told her what had happened, and she said, "Goddamn it. I wondered why I woke up with brown stains on my pillow."

According to the story I walked in on late, Thanksgiving had been a relatively good night for Gretchen. One morning a few weeks after the turkey episode, she walked into her kitchen in North Carolina and found on the countertop an open jam jar with crumbs in it. At first she thought they were from a cookie. Then she saw the overturned box and realized she had eaten something intended for her painted turtles. It was a nutrition bar, maybe four inches long and made of dead flies, pressed together the way Duraflame logs are. "Not only that," she said, "but when I was through, I ate all the petals off my poinsettia." She shook her head. "I noticed it on the counter next to the turtle-food box, and it was just a naked stalk."

I returned to my office more convinced than ever that this would be our last Christmas together. I mean, flies! If you're going to eat your pets' food in your sleep, why not think preventatively and exchange your turtles for a hamster or a rabbit, something safe and vegetarian? Get rid of the house-plants while you're at it—starting with the cactus—and lock up your cleaning supplies.

Later that evening, I found the sisters stretched out like cats in front of the woodstove. "It used to be that whenever I passed a mirror, I'd look at my face," Gretchen said, blowing out a mouthful of cigarette smoke. "Now I just check to see if my nipples line up."

Oh my God, I thought. *When did that start happening?* The last time we were all together for Christmas was 1994. We were at Gretchen's house in Raleigh, and she started the day by feeding her bullfrog, who was around the same size as her iron and was named Pappy. He was kept in a murky, heated thirty-gallon aquarium on her living room floor, next to three Japanese newts who lived in a meatloaf pan. It was a far cry from a normal Christmas, but what with our mother recently dead, it seemed better to break with tradition and try something completely different: thus my sister's place, with its feel of a swamp rather than the house we had grown up in, which now felt freighted with too much history. Gretchen's waist-length hair has gone silver since that Christmas, and when she walks in her sleep, she limps a little. But then, we're all getting older.

*

On our first day together in Sussex, we piled into the Volvo and rode to the town with the thirty-seven antique stores. Hugh drove, and I crawled into the way-back, thinking happily, *Here we are again, me and my sisters in a station wagon, just like when we were young.* Who would have imagined in 1966 that we'd one day be riding through southern England, none of us having realized the futures we'd predicted for ourselves? Amy was not the policewoman she'd so hoped to become. Lisa was not a nurse. No one had a houseful of servants or a trained proboscis monkey, yet we'd turned out OK, hadn't we?

In one of the antique stores we visited that afternoon, we saw a barrister's wig. It was foul, all the colors of dirty underpants, but that didn't stop Amy, and then Gretchen, from trying it on.

"That's OK," Lisa said when it was handed to her. "I don't want to get y'all's germs on my head."

Their germs, I thought.

The sun set at around four that afternoon, and it was dark by the time we headed home. I fell asleep in the way-back for a few minutes, and when I awoke, Lisa was discussing her uterus, specifically her fear that its lining may have grown too thick.

"What on earth gives you that idea?" Amy asked.

Lisa then mentioned a friend of hers, saying that if it could happen to Cynthia, it could just as easily happen to her. "Or to any of us," she said.

"And what if it does?" Gretchen asked. "Then we'll have to get them scraped out," Lisa reported.

I lifted my head over the backseat. "What's a uterus lined with, anyway?" I imagined something sweet and viscous. "Like whatever it is that grapes are made of."

"That would be grape," Amy said. "Grapes are made of grape."

"Actually, it's a good question," Lisa said. "What *is* a uterus lined with? Blood vessels? Nerves?"

"Your family," Hugh said. "I can't believe the things you talk about when you're together."

I later reminded him of the time his sister, Ann, visited us in Normandy. I walked into the living room after returning from a bike ride one afternoon and heard her saying to her mother, Joan, who was also staying with us, "Don't you just love the feel of an iguana?"

Who are you people? I remember thinking. That same night, after my bath, I overheard her asking, "Well, can't you make it with camel butter?"

"You can," Mrs. Hamrick said, "but I wouldn't recommend it."

I thought of asking for details—"Make *what* with camel butter?"—but decided I preferred the mystery. That often happens with company. I'll forever wonder what a guest from Paris meant when I walked into the yard one evening and heard her saying, "Mini goats might be nice." Or, odder still, when Hugh's father, Sam, came to visit with an old friend he'd known from the State Department. The two had been discussing the time they'd spent in Cameroon in the late sixties, and I entered the kitchen to hear Mr.

Hamrick say, "Now was that guy a Pygmy, or just a *false* Pygmy?"

I turned around and headed to my office, thinking, *I'll ask later.* Then Hugh's father died, as did his old friend from the State Department. I suppose I could Google "false Pygmy," but it wouldn't be the same. I had my chance to find out what one was, and I blew it.

One of Hugh's greatest regrets is that his father never saw the house in Sussex. It's the kind of place that was right up Sam's alley: a ruin transformed in such a way that it still looks pretty beat-up. The main difference is that now the wiring is safe, and there's heat. Mrs. Hamrick visits, though, and sometimes she and Hugh will sit in the kitchen and talk about Sam. It's not the snippets of conversation that betray him as the subject but rather their voices, which, almost a decade after his death, are still brittle and reverential, full of loss and longing. It's how my sisters and I used to be when talking about our mother. Now, though, after twenty-seven years, almost every discussion of her ends with the line "And can you believe she was so young?" Soon we'll be the age she was when she got cancer and was killed by it. Then we'll be even older, which just seems wrong, against nature somehow.

I made up my mind eons ago that I would not let that happen, that I would also die at sixty-two. Then I hit my mid-fifties and started thinking that perhaps I'm being a bit harsh. Now that I've scored a couple of decent guest rooms, it seems silly not to get a little more use out of them.

*

When visitors leave, I feel like an actor watching the audience file out of the theater, and it was no different with my sisters. The show over, Hugh and I returned to lesser versions of ourselves. We're not a horrible couple, but we have our share of fights, the type that can start with a misplaced sock and suddenly be about everything. "I haven't liked you since 2002," he hissed during a recent argument over which airport security line was moving the fastest.

This didn't hurt me so much as confuse me. "What happened in 2002?" I asked.

On the plane, he apologized, and a few weeks later, when I brought it up over dinner, he claimed to have no memory of it. That's one of Hugh's many outstanding qualities: he doesn't hold on to things. Another is that he's very good to old people, a group that in the not-too-distant future will include me. It's just this damned middle-aged period I have to get through.

The secret, of course, is to stay busy. So when the company leaves, I clean their bathrooms and strip their beds. If the guests were mine—my sisters, for example—I'll sit on the edge of the mattress and hold their sheets to my chest, hugging them a moment and breathing in their smell before standing back up and making my rickety way to that laundry room I always wanted.

Now We Are Five

In late May 2013, a few weeks shy of her fiftieth birthday, my youngest sister, Tiffany, committed suicide. She was living in a room in a beat-up house on the hard end of Somerville, Massachusetts, and had been dead, the coroner guessed, for at least five days before her door was battered down. I was given the news over a white courtesy phone while at the Dallas airport. Then, because my plane to Baton Rouge was boarding and I wasn't sure what else to do, I got on it. The following morning, I boarded another plane, this one to Atlanta, and the day after that I flew to Nashville, thinking all the while about my ever-shrinking family. A person expects his parents to die. But a sibling? I felt I'd lost the identity I'd enjoyed since 1968, when my brother was born. "Six kids!" people would say. "How do your poor folks manage?"

There were a lot of big families in the neighborhood I grew up in. Every other house was a fiefdom, so I never gave it much thought until I became an adult and my friends started having children. One or two seemed reasonable, but anything beyond that struck me as outrageous. A couple Hugh and I knew in Normandy would occasionally come to dinner with their wrecking crew of three, and when they'd leave several hours later every last part of me would feel violated.

Take those kids, double them, and subtract the cable TV: that's what my parents had to deal with. Now, though, there weren't six, only five. "And you can't really say, 'There *used* to be six,'" I told my sister Lisa. "It just makes people uncomfortable."

I recalled a father and son I'd met in California a few years back. "So are there other children?" I asked.

"There are," the man said. "Three who are living and a daughter, Chloe, who died before she was born, eighteen years ago."

That's not fair, I remember thinking. Because, I mean, what's a person supposed to do with *that?*

Compared to most forty-nine-year-olds, or even most forty-nine-*month*-olds, Tiffany didn't have much. She did leave a will, though. In it, she decreed that we, her family, could not have her body or attend her memorial service.

"So put *that* in your pipe and smoke it," our mother would

have said. A few days after getting the news, my sister Amy drove to Somerville with a friend and collected two boxes of things from Tiffany's room: family photos, many of which had been ripped into pieces; comment cards from a neighborhood grocery store; notebooks; receipts. The bed, a mattress on the floor, had been taken away and a large industrial fan had been set up. Amy snapped some pictures while she was there and, individually and in groups, those of us left studied them for clues: a paper plate on a dresser that had several drawers missing, a phone number written on a wall, a collection of mop handles, each one a different color, arranged like cattails in a barrel painted green.

Six months before our sister killed herself, I had made plans for us all to gather at a beach house on Emerald Isle, off the coast of North Carolina. My family used to vacation there every summer, but after my mother died we stopped going, not because we lost interest but because it was she who always made the arrangements and, more important, paid for it. The place I found with the help of my sister-in-law, Kathy, had six bedrooms and a small swimming pool. Our week-long rental period began on Saturday, June 8, and we arrived to find a delivery woman standing in the driveway with seven pounds of seafood, a sympathy gift sent by friends. "They's slaw in there too," she said, handing over the bags.

In the past, when my family rented a cottage, my sisters and I would crowd the door like puppies around a food dish. Our father would unlock it, and we'd tear through the house claiming rooms. I always picked the biggest one facing the ocean, and just as I'd start to unpack, my parents would enter and tell me that this was *theirs*. "I mean, just who the hell do you think you are?" my father would ask. He and my mother would move in, and I would get booted to what was called "the maid's room." It was always on the ground level, a kind of dank shed next to where the car was parked. There was never an interior stairway leading to the upper floor. Instead, I had to take the outside steps and, more often than not, knock on the locked front door like a beggar hoping to be invited in.

"What do *you* want?" my sisters would ask. "I want to come inside."

"That's funny," Lisa, the eldest, would say to the others, who were gathered like disciples around her. "Did you hear something, a whining sound? What is it that makes a noise like that? A hermit crab? A little sea slug?" Normally there was a social divide between the three oldest and three youngest children in my family. Lisa, Gretchen, and I treated the others like servants and did very well for ourselves. At the beach, though, all bets were off, and it was just upstairs against downstairs, meaning everyone against me.

This time, because I was paying, I got to choose the best room. Amy moved in next door, and my brother, Paul; his wife; and their ten-year-old daughter, Maddy, took the spot next to her. That was it for oceanfront. The others arrived later and had to take the leftovers. Lisa's room faced the street, as did my father's. Gretchen's faced the street and was intended for someone who was paralyzed. Hanging from the ceiling were electric pulleys designed to lift a harnessed body into and out of bed.

Unlike the cottages of our youth, this one did not have a maid's room. It was too new and fancy for that, as were the homes that surrounded it. Traditionally, the island houses were on stilts, but more and more often now the ground floors are filled in. They all have beachy names and are painted beachy colors, but most of those built after Hurricane Fran hit the coast in 1996 are three stories tall and look almost suburban. This place was vast and airy. The kitchen table sat twelve, and there was not one but *two* dishwashers. The pictures were ocean-related: seascapes and lighthouses, all with the airborne Vs that are shorthand for seagull. A sampler on the living room wall read OLD SHELLERS NEVER DIE, THEY SIMPLY CONCH OUT. On the round clock beside it, the numbers lay in an indecipherable heap, as if they'd come unglued. Just above them were printed the words WHO CARES?

This was what we found ourselves saying whenever anyone asked the time.

"Who cares?"

The day before we arrived at the beach, Tiffany's obituary ran in the *Raleigh News & Observer*. It was submitted by Gretchen, who stated that our sister had passed away peacefully at her home. This made it sound as if she were very old and had a house. But what else could you do? People were

17

leaving responses on the paper's website, and one fellow wrote that Tiffany used to come into the video store where he worked in Somerville. When his glasses broke, she offered him a pair she had found while foraging for art supplies in somebody's trash can. He said she also gave him a *Playboy* magazine from the 1960s that included a photo spread titled "The Ass Menagerie."

This was fascinating, as we didn't really know our sister very well. All of us had pulled away from the family at some point in our lives—we'd had to in order to forge our own identities, to go from being *a* Sedaris to our own specific Sedaris. Tiffany, though, stayed away. She might promise to come home for Christmas, but at the last minute there'd always be some excuse: she missed her plane, she had to work. The same would happen with our summer vacations. "The rest of us managed to make it," I'd say, aware of how old and guilt-trippy I sounded.

We'd all be disappointed by her absence, though for different reasons. Even if you weren't getting along with Tiffany at the time, you couldn't deny the show she put on—the dramatic entrances, the nonstop professional-grade insults, the chaos she'd inevitably leave in her wake. One day she'd throw a dish at you, and the next she'd create a mosaic made of the shards. When allegiances with one brother or sister flamed out, she'd take up with someone else. At no time did she get along with everybody, but there was always someone she was in contact with. Toward the end it was Lisa, but before that we'd all had our turn.

The last time she joined us on Emerald Isle was in 1986. "And, even then, she left after three days," Gretchen reminded us.

As kids, we spent our beach time swimming. Then we became teenagers and devoted ourselves to tanning. There's a certain kind of talk that takes place when you're lying, dazed, in the sun, and I've always been partial to it. On the first afternoon of our most recent trip, we laid out one of the bedspreads we'd had as children and arranged ourselves side by side on it, trading stories about Tiffany.

"What about the Halloween she spent on that Army base?"

"And the time she showed up at Dad's birthday party with a black eye?"

"I remember this girl she met years ago at a party," I began when my turn came. "She'd been talking about facial scars and how terrible it would be to have one, so Tiffany said, 'I have a little scar on my face and I don't think it's so awful.'

"'Well,' the girl said, 'you would if you were pretty.'"

Amy laughed and rolled over onto her stomach. "Oh, that's a good line!"

I rearranged the towel I was using as a pillow. "Isn't it, though?" Coming from someone else the story might have been upsetting, but not being pretty was never one of Tiffany's problems, especially when she was in her twenties and thirties, and men tumbled helpless before her.

"Funny," I said, "but I don't remember a scar on her face."

*

I stayed in the sun too long that day and got a burn on my forehead. That was basically it for me and the beach blanket. I made brief appearances for the rest of the week, stopping to dry off after a swim, but mainly I spent my days on a bike, cycling up and down the coast and thinking about what had happened. While the rest of us seem to get along effortlessly, with Tiffany it always felt like work. She and I usually made up after arguing, but our last fight took it out of me, and at the time of her death we hadn't spoken in eight years. During that period, I regularly found myself near Somerville, and though I'd always toy with the idea of contacting her, I never did, despite my father's encouragement. Meanwhile I'd get reports from him and Lisa: Tiffany had lost her apartment, had gone on disability, had moved into a room found for her by a social service agency. Perhaps she was more forthcoming with her friends, but her family got things only in bits and pieces. She didn't talk *with* us so much as *at* us, great blocks of speech that were by turns funny, astute, and so contradictory it was hard to connect the sentence you were hearing with the one that preceded it. Before we stopped speaking I could always tell when she was on the phone. I'd walk into the house and hear Hugh say, "Uh-huh ... uh-huh ... uh-huh ... "

In addition to the two boxes that Amy had filled in Somerville, she also brought down our sister's 1978 ninth-grade yearbook. Among the messages inscribed by her class-mates was the following, written by someone who had drawn a marijuana leaf beside her name:

*Tiffany. You are a one-of-a-kind girl so stay that way
you unique ass. I'm only sorry we couldn't have partied
more together. This school sux to hell. Stay*
-cool
-stoned
-drunk
-fucked-up
Check your ass later.

Then there's:

Tiffany,

*I'm looking forward to getting high with you
this summer.*

Tiffany,

*Call me sometime this summer and we'll go out and
get blitzed.*

A few weeks after these messages were written, Tiffany
ran away and was subsequently sent to a disciplinary institution in Maine called Élan. According to what she told us
later, it was a horrible place. She returned home in 1980,
having spent two years there, and from that point on none
of us can recall a conversation in which she did not mention
it. She blamed the family for sending her off, but we, her

21

siblings, had nothing to do with it. Paul, for instance, was ten when she left. I was twenty-one. For a year, I sent her monthly letters. Then she wrote and told me to stop. As for my parents, there were only so many times they could apologize. "We had other kids," they said in their defense. "You think we could let the world stop on account of any one of you?"

We were at the beach for three days before Lisa and our father, who is now ninety, joined us. Being on the island meant missing the spinning classes he takes in Raleigh, so I found a fitness center not far from the rental cottage, and every afternoon he and I would spend some time there. On the way over we'd talk to each other, but as soon as we mounted our stationary bikes we'd each retreat in to our own thoughts. It was a small place, not very lively. A mute television oversaw the room, tuned to the Weather Channel and reminding us that there's always a catastrophe somewhere or other, always someone flooded from his home or running for his life from a funnel-shaped cloud. Toward the end of the week, I came upon my father in Amy's room, sifting through the photos that Tiffany had destroyed. In his hand was a fragment of my mother's head with a patch of blue sky behind her. *Under what circumstances had this been ripped up?* I wondered. It seemed such a melodramatic gesture, like throwing a glass against a wall. Something someone in a movie would do.

"Just awful," my father whispered. "A person's life

reduced to one lousy box." I put my hand on his shoulder. "Actually there are two of them."

He corrected himself. "Two lousy boxes."

One afternoon on Emerald Isle, we all rode to the Food Lion for groceries. I was in the produce department, looking at red onions, when my brother sneaked up from behind and let loose with a loud "Achoo," this while whipping a bouquet of wet parsley through the air. I felt the spray on the back of my neck and froze, thinking a very sick stranger had just sneezed on me. It's a neat trick, but he also doused the Indian woman who was standing to my left. She was wearing a blood-colored sari, so she got it on her bare arm as well as her neck and the lower part of her back.

"Sorry, man," Paul said when she turned around, horrified. "I was just playing a joke on my brother."

The woman had many thin bracelets on, and they jangled as she brushed her hand against the back of her head.

"You called her 'man,'" I said to him after she walked off. "For real?" he asked.

Amy mimicked him perfectly. "For real?"

Over the phone, my brother, like me, is often mistaken for a woman. As we continued shopping, he told us that his van had recently broken down and that when he called for a tow truck the dispatcher said, "We'll be right out, sweetie." He lowered a watermelon into the cart and turned to his daughter. "Maddy's got a daddy who talks like a lady, but she don't care, do she?" Giggling, she punched him in the stomach, and I was struck by how comfortable the two of them are with each other. Our father was a figure of authority, while Paul is more of a playmate.

When we went to the beach as children, on or about the fourth day, our father would say, "Wouldn't it be nice to buy a cottage down here?" We'd get our hopes up, and then he would bring practical concerns into it. They weren't petty—buying a house that will eventually get blown away by a hurricane probably isn't the best way to spend your money—but still we wanted one desperately. I told myself when I was young that one day *I* would buy a beach house and that it would be everyone's, as long as they followed my draconian rules and never stopped thanking me for it. Thus it was that on Wednesday morning, midway through our vacation, Hugh and I contacted a real estate agent named Phyllis, who took us around to look at available properties. On Friday afternoon, we made an offer on an oceanfront cottage not far from the one we were renting, and before sunset our bid was accepted. I made the announcement at the dinner table and got the reaction I had expected.

"Now, wait a minute," my father said. "You need to think clearly here."

"I already have," I told him.

"OK, then, how old is the roof? How many times has it been replaced in the last ten years?"

"When can we move in?" Gretchen asked.

Lisa wanted to know if she could bring her dogs, and Amy asked what the house was named.

"Right now it's called Fantastic Place," I told her, "but we're going to change it." I used to think the ideal name for a beach house was the Ship Shape. Now, though, I had a better idea. "We're going to call it the Sea Section."

My father put down his hamburger. "Oh no, you're not."

"But it's perfect," I argued. "The name's supposed to be beachy, and if it's a pun, all the better."

I brought up a cottage we'd seen earlier in the day called Dune Our Thing, and my father winced. "How about naming it Tiffany?" he said.

Our silence translated to: *Let's pretend we didn't hear that.*

He picked his hamburger back up. "I think it's a great idea. The perfect way to pay our respects."

"If that's the case we could name it after Mom," I told him. "Or half after Tiffany and half after Mom. But it's a house, not a tombstone, and it wouldn't fit in with the names of the other houses."

"Aw, baloney," my father said. "Fitting in—that's not who we are. That's not what we're about."

Paul interrupted to nominate the Conch Sucker.

Amy's suggestion had the word "Seaman" in it, and Gretchen's was even dirtier.

"What's wrong with the name it already has?" Lisa asked. "No, no, no," my father said, forgetting, I think, that this wasn't his decision. A few days later, after the buyer's remorse had kicked in, I'd wonder if I hadn't bought the house as a way of saying, *See, it's just that easy. No hemming and hawing. No asking to look at the septic tank. Rather, you make your family happy and iron out the details later.* The cottage we bought is two stories tall and was built in 1978. It's on proper stilts and has two rear decks, one above the other, overlooking the ocean. It was rented to vacationers until late September, but Phyllis allowed us to drop by and show it to the family the following morning, after we checked out of the house we'd been staying in. A place always looks different—worse, most often—after you've made the commitment to buy it, so while the others raced up and down the stairs, claiming their future bedrooms, I held my nose to a vent and caught a whiff of mildew. The sale included the furniture, so I also made an inventory of the Barcaloungers and massive TVs I would eventually be getting rid of, along with the shell-patterned bedspreads and cushions with anchors on them. "For our beach house, I want to have a train theme," I announced. "Trains on the curtains, trains on the towels—we're going to go all out."

"Oh brother," my father moaned.

We sketched a plan to return for Thanksgiving, and after saying goodbye to one another, my family splintered into groups and headed off to our respective homes. There'd been a breeze at the beach house, but once we left the island the air grew still. As the heat intensified, so did the general feeling of depression. Throughout the sixties and seventies, the road back to Raleigh took us past Smithfield and a billboard on the outskirts of town that read WELCOME TO KLAN COUNTRY. This time we took a different route, one my brother recommended. Hugh drove, and my father sat beside him. I slumped down in the backseat next to Amy, and every time I raised my head, I'd see the same soybean field or low-slung cinder-block building we'd seemingly passed twenty minutes earlier.

We'd been on the road for a little more than an hour when we stopped at a farmers' market. Inside an open-air pavilion, a woman offered complimentary plates of hummus served with a corn and black-bean salad, so we each accepted one and took seats on a bench. Twenty years earlier, the most a place like this might have offered was fried okra. Now there was organic coffee and artisanal goat cheese. Above our heads hung a sign that read WHISPERING DOVE RANCH, and just as I thought that we might be anywhere, I noticed that the music piped through the speakers was Christian—the new kind, which says that Jesus is awesome.

Hugh brought my father a plastic cup of water. "You OK, Lou?"

"Fine," my father answered.

"Why do you think she did it?" I asked as we stepped back into the sunlight. For that's all any of us were thinking, *had been* thinking, since we got the news. Mustn't Tiffany have hoped that whatever pills she'd taken wouldn't be strong enough and that her failed attempt would lead her back into our fold? How could anyone purposefully leave us—*us*, of all people? This is how I thought of it, for though I've often lost faith in myself, I've never lost faith in my family, in my certainty that we are fundamentally better than everyone else. It's an archaic belief, one I haven't seriously reconsidered since my late teens, but still I hold it. Ours is the only club I'd ever wanted to be a member of, so I couldn't imagine quitting. Backing off for a year or two was understandable, but to want out so badly that you'd take your own life?

"I don't know that it had anything to do with us," my father said. But how could it have not? Doesn't the blood of every suicide splash back on our faces?

At the far end of the parking lot was a stand selling reptiles. In giant tanks were two pythons, each as big around as a fire hose. The heat seemed to suit them, and I watched as they raised their heads, testing the screened ceilings. Beside the snakes was a low pen corralling an alligator with its mouth banded shut. It wasn't full-grown but perhaps an adolescent, around three feet long and grumpy-looking. A girl had stuck her arm through the wire and was stroking the thing's back while it glared, seething. "I'd like to buy everything here just so I could kill it," I said.

My father mopped his forehead with a Kleenex. "I'm with you, brother."

When we were young and would set off for the beach, I'd look out the window at all the landmarks we drove by—the Purina silo on the south side of Raleigh, the Klan billboard—knowing that when we passed them a week later, I'd be miserable. Our vacation over, now there'd be nothing to live for until Christmas. My life is much fuller than it was back then, yet this return felt no different. "What time is it?" I asked Amy.

And instead of saying "Who cares?" she snapped, "You tell me. You're the one with a watch on."

At the airport a few hours later, I picked sand from my pockets and thought of our final moments at the beach house I'd bought. I was on the front porch with Phyllis, who had just locked the door, and we turned to see the others in the driveway below us. "So is that one of your sisters?" she asked, pointing to Gretchen.

"It is," I said. "And so are the two women standing on either side of her."

"Then you've got your brother," she observed. "That makes five—wow. Now, *that's* a big family."

I looked at the sunbaked cars we would soon be climbing into—furnaces, every one of them—and said, "Yes. It certainly is."

Little Guy

I was sitting around the house one evening when I suddenly wondered how tall Rock Hudson was. It's not often that I think of him, but I'd recently rewatched the movie *Giant,* so he was on my mind.

One of the many things I'll never understand is why a search on my computer might be different from a search on someone else's—my sister Amy's, for instance. She'll go to Google, type in "What does a fifty-year-old woman look like?," and summon pictures I can't believe they allow on the Internet, unlocked, where just anyone can see them. I don't mean *Playboy* shots but the sort you'd find in *Hustler*. It's as if she'd asked, "What does *the inside* of a fifty-year-old woman look like?" I did the same search and got pictures of Meg Ryan and Brooke Shields, smiling.

I said to Hugh, "This computer of mine is so ... wholesome."

I said it again after looking up Rock Hudson. "How tall is ... " I began, and before I could finish, Google interrupted me with " ... Jesus? You want to know how tall Jesus was?"

Well, OK, I thought. *But it's Rock Hudson I was really curious about.*

Were Amy to open her laptop and type "How tall is ... " Google would finish her question with " ... Tom Hardy's dick?" With mine, though, it's Jesus, who they're guessing came in at around six feet, which is ridiculous in my opinion. What are the odds that he was both tall *and* handsome? Is he described that way in the Bible? In some of the early northern European paintings, Christ looks like you flushed him out from under a bridge, but in Sunday-school books and the sorts of pictures they sell at Christian supply stores, he falls somewhere between Kenny Loggins and Jared Leto, always doe-eyed and, of course, white, with brown—not black—hair, usually wavy. And he always has a fantastic body, shown at its best on the cross, which—face it—was practically designed to make a man's stomach and shoulders look good.

What would happen, I often wonder, if someone sculpted a morbidly obese Jesus with titties and acne scars, and hair on his back? On top of that, he should be short—five foot two at most. "Sacrilege!" people would shout. But why?

Doing good deeds doesn't make you good-looking. Take Jimmy Carter. Habitat for Humanity didn't do a thing for those tombstone-size teeth of his. Or at least I remember his teeth as seeming pretty big. I should Google Image them. On Amy's computer.

At five-five, I never give much thought to my height until I do. Whenever I come across a man my size—at the airport, say, or in a hotel lobby—I squeak the way a one-year-old does when it spots a fellow baby. It's all I can do not to toddle over and embrace the guy. Whenever I *do* say something—"Look, we're the same height!"—it turns weird, though I don't know why. Don't fellow Porsche drivers acknowledge one another, or people walking the same breed of dog? With small straight men, I often get the feeling that they don't want their shortness pointed out, that it's like saying, "Look, I have a bald spot too!"

I want to ask the guys my size if, like me, they find themselves being hit up for money a lot. Hugh and I will walk through one city or another and, while he'll advance down the sidewalk uninterrupted, I'll get stopped again and again. "Can you give me a dollar? A cigarette? Whatever's in that bag you're holding?"

It's not that I have a particularly friendly face, so I have to assume that my stature has something to do with it, especially when the request becomes a demand. "I *said*, 'Give me a dollar.'"

"Would you be talking to me this way if I were taller than you?" I want to ask the ten-year-old with his hand out.

I know that short straight men sometimes have it hard when it comes to finding a girlfriend, but I thought that for people like myself—"pocket gays," we're sometimes called—it was no hindrance. In retrospect, I guess I wasn't paying much attention. The *Washington Post* has a regular feature in which they send two people out on a date and then check in to see how it went. Recently the couple was gay. Both stood more than six feet and listed in their "Deal-Breakers" box "short men." They did not, I noticed, exclude white supremacists or machine-gun owners.

Who wants to date you anyway? I wondered, scowling at the photos.

I'm not one of those short men who feels he got shafted. Yes, it's hard to buy things off the rack, but that's what tailors are for. I fit easily into airplane seats. I can blend into crowds when I want to. Added height would be of no more use to me than a square head, so who needs it? I like knowing how tall other people are, though, especially celebrities. That's why I Googled Rock Hudson, who, at six foot five, had every right to appear in *Giant*. He towered over his costars in that picture, but with other actors it's hard to tell.

I once asked someone in the movie business how tall Paul Newman was. This was back when he was still alive and before I had the Internet. "Oh," said this woman who'd worked with him on *Mr. & Mrs. Bridge,* "he's tiny."

"What does that mean?"

"He's a shrimp," the woman said. "In photos he seems

average enough, but in real life you practically need a microscope to see him."

"So he's, like, the size of a flu germ?"

"Just about," she said. "I'd put him at around five-nine."

"I'm four inches shorter," I told her, "so what does that make me?"

"Well ... you know," she said.

Before I learned to never, under any circumstances, read anything about myself, I'd occasionally stumble upon an interview I'd given. Then I'd recall the journalist who wrote it and mistakenly wonder what his or her writing was like. In Australia a few years back, I was surprised when a woman I'd very much enjoyed talking to described me as "bonsai-size." This didn't offend me. Rather, I was taken aback. She might have been an inch or two taller than me, but it's not like I came to her knees or anything. I've been called "diminutive" as well, and "elfin," as if I sleep in a teacup.

A few years ago I opened a paper in Ottawa and saw that the journalist I'd spoken to the day before had described me as "slight and effeminate." *Really?* I thought. The first adjective seemed fair enough, but the second one threw me. I know I cross my legs a lot, but I don't think my walk is especially ladylike. I don't wave my hands around when I talk or address anyone as "Miss Thing." In the end I decided the word was more about him than it was about me. But isn't it often that way?

It's one thing for someone to describe you in print, to go through several drafts and, after careful consideration, choose the adjective "Lilliputian" over, say, "pint-size." It's another thing when they blurt it out. "You horrible little man," an Englishwoman once said after I'd written something she didn't like in her book. In 1987, while I was home for Christmas, my sister Tiffany got into a fight with my sister Gretchen. I came in at the very end, just as it was breaking up, and when I asked what was going on, Tiffany said, "Why don't you go back to your room and write some more about being a faggot?"

How long has that *been in there?* I wondered. It's scary the things that come out when you're mad at someone. Some years back at a small airport in Wisconsin, a TSA agent ordered me to take off my vest. "I've been wearing this for three weeks," I told her. "Every day I've traveled to a different city, and this is the first time I've been asked to remove it."

The woman was maybe ten years older than me, which at the time would have put her in her early sixties. Her dyed hair was cut short and was carefully styled in a way that made me think of chocolate cake frosting. "I want it off *now!*" she barked.

"It must be nice to hold such an important position," I wanted to say as I started undoing the buttons. Then I thought of how snobbish that sounded and was ashamed of myself. Here I was, angry, and my first instinct was to attack her job—her class, really. *Have I always been this person?* I wondered as I walked through the archway in my stocking feet. What does it mean that my second option, "I'm so glad you're not *my* grandmother," wasn't much better?

I later wondered how this woman might have described me and realized that all she needed to say was "the jerk in the vest." Actually, in this context, the word "jerk" is unnecessary. As with "the guy in the white boots," I think it's already implied. I mean, really, *a vest!* What was I thinking? It wasn't the kind that came with a suit but rather a "worker's vest," modeled on one from the nineteenth century, with pockets for all my mule-skinning tools.

She also might have described me as "the gay guy." While this doesn't bother me, I don't think of it as the cornerstone of what I am. Given all my current options, I think I prefer "the little guy." Who wants to waste his time bothering a person like that? So tiny. So inconsequential. A speck.

Stepping Out

I was at an Italian restaurant in Melbourne, listening as a woman named Lesley talked about her housekeeper, an immigrant to Australia who earlier that day had cleaned the bathroom countertops with a bottle of very expensive acne medication: "She's afraid of the vacuum cleaner and can't read or write a word of English, but other than that she's marvelous."

Lesley works for a company that goes into developing countries and trains doctors to remove cataracts. "It's incredibly rewarding," she said as our antipasto plate arrived. "These are people who've been blind for years, and suddenly, miraculously, they can see again." She brought up a man who'd been operated on in a remote area of China.

"They took off the bandages, and for the first time in two decades he saw his wife. Then he opened his mouth and said, 'You're so . . . old.'"

Lesley pushed back her shirtsleeve, and as she reached for an olive, I noticed a rubber bracelet on her left wrist. "Is that a watch?" I asked.

"No," she told me. "It's a Fitbit. You sync it with your computer, and it tracks your physical activity."

I leaned closer, and as she tapped the thickest part of it, a number of glowing dots rose to the surface and danced back and forth. "It's like a pedometer," she continued, "but updated, and better. The goal is to take ten thousand steps per day, and once you do, it vibrates."

I forked some salami into my mouth. "Hard?"

"No," she said. "It's just a tingle."

A few weeks later I bought a Fitbit of my own and discovered what she was talking about. Ten thousand steps, I learned, amounts to a little more than four miles for someone my size. It sounds like a lot, but you can cover that distance over the course of an average day without even trying, especially if you have stairs in your house and a steady flow of people who regularly knock, wanting you to accept a package or give them directions or just listen patiently as they talk about birds, which happens from time to time when I'm home in West Sussex. One April afternoon the person at my door hoped to sell me a wooden bench. It was bought, he said, for a client whose garden he was designing. "Last week she loved it, but now she's decided to go with something else." In the bright sunlight, the fellow's hair was as orange as a Popsicle. "The company I ordered it from has a no-return policy, so I'm wondering if maybe *you'd* like to buy it." He gestured toward an unmarked van idling in front of the house and seemed angry when I told him that I wasn't interested. "You could at least take a look before making up your mind," he said.

I closed the door a couple of inches. "That's OK." Then, because it's an excuse that works for just about everything, I added, "I'm American."

"Meaning?" he said.

"We . . . stand up a lot," I told him.

"Oldest trick in the book," my neighbor Thelma said when I told her what had happened. "That bench was stolen from someone's garden, I guarantee it."

This was seconded by the fellow who came to empty our septic tank. "Pikeys," he said.

"Come again?"

"Tinkers," he said. "Pikeys."

"That means Gypsies," Thelma explained, adding that the politically correct word is "travelers."

I was traveling myself when I got my Fitbit, and because the tingle feels so good, not just as a sensation but also as a mark of accomplishment, I began pacing the airport rather than doing what I normally do, which is sit in the waiting area, wondering which of the many people around me will die first, and of what. I also started taking the stairs instead of the escalator and avoiding the moving sidewalk. "Every little bit helps," my old friend Dawn, who frequently eats lunch while hula-hooping and has been known to visit her local Y three times a day, said. She had a Fitbit as well, and swore by it. Others I met weren't quite so taken. These were people who had worn one until the battery died. Then, instead of recharging it, which couldn't be simpler, they'd stuck it in a drawer, most likely with all the other devices they'd lost interest in over the years. To people like Dawn and me, people who are obsessive to begin with, the Fitbit is a digital trainer, perpetually egging us on. During the first few weeks that I had it, I'd return to my hotel at the end of the day, and when I discovered that I'd taken a total of, say, twelve thousand steps, I'd go out for another three thousand.

"But why?" Hugh asked when I told him about it. "Why isn't twelve thousand enough?"

"Because," I told him, "my Fitbit thinks I can do better."

I look back at that time and laugh—fifteen thousand steps—ha! That's only about seven miles! Not bad if you're on a business trip or you're just getting used to a prosthetic leg. In Sussex, though, it's nothing. Our house is situated on the edge of a rolling downland, a perfect position if you like what the English call "rambling." I'll follow a trail every now and then, but as a rule I prefer roads, partly because it's harder to get lost on a road but mainly because I'm afraid of snakes. The only venomous ones in England are adders, and even though they're hardly ubiquitous, I've seen three that had been run over by cars. Then I met a woman named

Janine who was bitten and had to spend a week in the hospital. "It was completely my own fault," she said. "I shouldn't have been wearing sandals."

"It didn't *have* to strike you," I reminded her. "It could have just slid away."

Janine was the type who'd likely blame herself for getting mugged. "It's what I get for having anything worth taking!" she'd probably say. At first, I found her attitude fascinating. Then I got vindictive on her behalf and started carrying a snake killer, or at least something that could be used to grab one by the neck and fling it into the path of an oncoming car. It's a hand-sized claw on a pole and was originally designed for picking up litter. With it, I can walk, fear snakes a little less, and satisfy my insane need for order all at the same time. I'd been cleaning the roads in my area of Sussex for three years, but before the Fitbit I did it primarily on my bike, and with my bare hands. That was fairly effective, but I wound up missing a lot. On foot, nothing escapes my attention: a potato-chip bag stuffed into the hollow of a tree, an elderly mitten caught in the embrace of a blackberry bush, a mud-coated matchbook at the bottom of a ditch. Then there's all the obvious stuff: the cans and bottles and great greasy sheets of paper fish-and-chips come wrapped in. You can tell where my territory ends and the rest of England begins. It's like going from the Rose Garden in Sissinghurst to Fukushima after the tsunami. The difference is staggering.

*

Since getting my Fitbit I've seen all kinds of things I wouldn't normally have come across. Once it was a toffee-colored cow with two feet sticking out of her. I was rambling that afternoon with my friend Maja, and as she ran to inform the farmer, I marched in place, envious of the extra steps she was getting in. Given all the time I've spent in the country, you'd think I might have seen a calf being born, but this was a first for me. The biggest surprise was how nonplussed the expectant mother was. For a while she lay flat on the grass, panting. Then she got up and began grazing, still with those feet sticking out.

"Really?" I said to her. "You can't go *five minutes* without eating?"

Around her were other cows, all of whom seemed blind to her condition.

"Do you think she knows there's a baby at the end of this?" I asked Maja after she'd returned. "A woman is told what's going to happen in the delivery room, but how does an animal interpret this pain?"

I thought of the first time I had a kidney stone. That was in New York, in 1991, back when I had no money or health insurance. All I knew was that I was hurting and couldn't afford to do anything about it. The night was spent moaning. Then I peed blood, followed by what looked like a piece of gravel from an aquarium. That's when I put it all together.

What might I have thought if, after seven hours of unrelenting agony, a creature the size of a full-grown cougar emerged inch by inch from the hole at the end of my penis and started hassling me for food? Was that what the cow was going through? Did she think she was dying, or had instinct somehow prepared her for this? Maja and I watched for an hour. Then the sun started to set and we trekked on, disappointed. I left for London the next day, and when I returned several weeks later and hiked back to the field, I saw mother and child standing side by side, not in the loving way I had imagined but more like strangers waiting for the post office to open.

Other animals I've seen on my walks are foxes and rabbits. I've stumbled upon deer, stoats, a hedgehog, and more pheasant than I could possibly count. All the badgers I find are dead, run over by cars and eventually feasted upon by carrion-eating slugs, which are themselves eventually flattened and feasted upon by other slugs.

Back when Maja and I saw the cow, I was averaging twenty-five thousand steps, or around ten and a half miles per day. Trousers that had grown too snug were suddenly loose again, and I noticed that my face was looking a lot thinner. Then I upped it to thirty thousand steps and started walking farther afield. "We saw David in Arundel picking up a dead squirrel with his grabbers," the neighbors told Hugh. "We saw him outside Steyning rolling a tire down the side of the road," " . . . in Pulborough dislodging a pair of Y-fronts from a tree branch." Before the Fitbit, once we'd eaten dinner, I was in for the evening. Now, though, as soon as I'm finished with the dishes, I walk to the pub and back, a distance of 3,895 steps. There are no streetlights where we live, and the houses I pass at eleven p.m. are either dark or very dimly lit. I often hear owls and the flapping of wood-cocks disturbed by the beam of my flashlight. One night I heard a creaking sound and noticed that the minivan parked a dozen or so steps ahead of me was rocking back and forth. A lot of people where we live seem to have sex in their cars. I know this because I find their used condoms, sometimes on the road but more often just off it, in little pull-over areas. In addition to spent condoms, in one of the spots that I patrol, I regularly pick up empty KFC containers and a great number of soiled Handi Wipes. *Do they eat fried chicken and then have sex, or is it the other way around?* I wonder.

I look back on the days I averaged only thirty thousand steps and think, *Honestly, how lazy can you get?* When I hit thirty-five thousand steps a day, Fitbit sent me an e-badge, and then one for forty thousand, and forty-five thousand. Now I'm up to sixty thousand, which is twenty-five and a half miles. Walking that distance at the age of fifty-seven with completely flat feet while lugging a heavy bag of garbage takes close to nine hours—a big block of time but hardly wasted. I listen to audiobooks and pod-casts. I talk to people. I learn things: the fact, for example, that in the days of yore, peppercorns were sold individually, and because they were so valuable, to guard against theft, the people who packed them had to have their pockets sewn shut.

At the end of my first sixty-thousand-step day, I staggered home with my flashlight knowing that now I'd advance to sixty-five thousand and that there'd be no end to it until my feet snapped off at the ankles. Then it'd just be my jagged bones stabbing into the soft ground. Why is it some people can manage a thing like a Fitbit, while others go off the rails and allow it to rule, and perhaps even ruin, their lives? While marching along the roadside, I often think of a TV show that I watched a few years back—*Obsessed,* it was called. One of the episodes was devoted to a woman who owned two treadmills and walked like a hamster on a wheel from the moment she got up until she went to bed. Her family would eat dinner and she'd observe them from her vantage point beside the table, panting as she asked her children about their day. I knew that I was supposed to scoff at this woman—to be, at the very least, entertainingly disgusted, the way I am with the people on *Hoarders*—but instead I saw something of myself in her. Of course, she did her walking on a treadmill, where it served no greater purpose. So it's not like we're *really* that much alike. Is it?

In recognition of all the rubbish I've collected since getting my Fitbit, my local council is naming a garbage truck after me. The fellow in charge emailed to ask which font I would like my name written in, and I answered, "Roman."

"Get it?" I said to Hugh. *"Roamin'."*

He lost patience with me somewhere around the thirty-five-thousand mark and responded with a heavy sigh.

Shortly after I decided on a typeface, for reasons I cannot

determine, my Fitbit died. I was devastated when I tapped the broadest part of it and the little dots failed to appear. Then I felt a great sense of freedom. It seemed that my life was now my own again. But was it? Walking twenty-five miles, or even running up the stairs and back, suddenly seemed pointless, since without the steps being counted and registered, what use were they? I lasted five hours before I ordered a replacement, express delivery. It arrived the following afternoon, and my hands shook as I tore open the box. Ten minutes later, my new master strapped securely around my left wrist, I was out the door, racing, practically running, to make up for lost time.

A House Divided

Because I'd accumulated so many miles, they bumped me to first class on the flight from Atlanta to Raleigh. I had assumed that our plane would be on the small side, but instead, owing to Thanksgiving and the great number of travelers, it was full-size. I was seated in the second row, in front of a woman who looked to be in her early sixties and was letting her hair fade from dyed red to gray. After she'd settled in she started a conversation with the fellow beside her. That's how I learned that she lived in Costa Rica. "It's on account of my husband," she said. "He's military, well, *retired* military, though you never really leave the Marine Corps, do you?"

She started explaining what had taken her from North

Carolina to Central America, but then the flight attendant came to take a drink order from the guy next to me, and I missed it. Just as I was tuning back in, a man across the aisle tried to open his overhead bin. It was stuck for some reason and he pounded on it, saying to anyone who would listen, "This is like Obamacare: broken."

Several of the passengers around me laughed, and I noted their faces, vowing that in the event of a crisis, I would not help lead them to an emergency exit. *You people are on your own,* I thought, knowing that if anything bad *did* happen, it would likely be one of them who'd save me. It would be just my luck. I had passed judgment, so fate would force me to eat my words.

After we took off from Atlanta I pulled out my notebook, half making a list of things we'd need for Thanksgiving and half listening to the woman behind me, who continued to talk throughout the entire flight. I guessed she was drinking, though I could have been wrong. Perhaps she was always this loud and adamant. "I never said I'd spend the rest of my *life* there, that's not what I meant *at all.*"

It was dark by the time we landed in Raleigh, and as we taxied to the gate, one of the flight attendants made an announcement. The "remain seated until the FASTEN SEAT BELT sign has been turned off" part was to be expected, but then she added that we had some very special passengers on board.

Oh no, I thought. *Please don't embarrass me.* I was just wondering who the other important person might be when she said, "With us today is the outstanding soccer team from ..." She named a high school in the Triangle Area and concluded with, "Let's give them all a great big hand!"

The woman behind me whooped and cheered, and when no one joined her, she raised her voice, shouting, "You people are ... *assholes!* I mean, what the hell, you can't even applaud for your own *teenagers?*"

I'd meant to but figured the team was back in coach. They wouldn't have heard me one way or the other, so what difference did it make?

"Pathetic," the woman spat. "Too wrapped up in your ... smartphones and iPads to congratulate a group of high school athletes."

You couldn't say she hadn't nailed us. Still I had to bite my hand to keep from laughing. It's so funny to be called an asshole by someone who doesn't know you, but then again knows you so perfectly.

"See that woman?" I said to Hugh when he met me at the baggage claim a few minutes later.

I told him what had happened on the plane, and he folded his arms across his chest, the way he always does before lecturing me. "She was right, you know. You should have applauded."

"We've been apart for two months," I reminded him. "Would it kill you to take my side in this?"

He apologized, but after I'd wrestled my bag off the carousel and we'd started toward the parking lot, he added quietly, but not so quietly that I couldn't hear him, "You really should have clapped." From the airport we drove to my brother Paul's. There we met up with my sister Gretchen, who had a cast on her right forearm and held it aloft, like someone perpetually being sworn in. "It helps ease the pain," she explained.

I hadn't seen Gretchen since the previous spring and was startled by her appearance. For as long as I could remember she'd worn her hair long, and though it still fell to below her shoulder blades in the back, the top was now cropped and stood from the crown of her head like the fur of a graying German shepherd. Odder still, she had a sun visor on. "Since when have you had this mullet?" I asked.

Only when she lifted it off did I realize she was wearing a cap, the sort sold in joke shops. "The hair is attached to the top of it. See? I got it at the beach last month."

I hadn't been to our house on Emerald Isle—the Sea Section—since we'd bought it five months earlier, though Hugh had. He'd flown over in late September to start making improvements. Gretchen joined him for a few days shortly before Halloween and fell into a rut while walking on the beach. That's how she broke her arm. "Can you believe it?" she asked. "No one has worse luck than me."

When there's no traffic, it's a two-and-a-half-hour drive from Raleigh to Emerald Isle. We left at around eight p.m., and on the way, I asked Gretchen about her job. She works as a horticulturalist for the city of Raleigh and had recently discovered a campsite in one of its larger parks. That's common enough, but this one was occupied by someone we once knew. His name was familiar, but I couldn't picture his face until Gretchen put him in context. "He used to come over to the house and hang out with Mom."

"Oh, right," I said.

Kids like to believe that their parents will get lonely after they leave the house, but I think my mother actually did. She delighted in her children and always enjoyed talking to our friends and the people we were going out with. "Why don't you invite Jeff to dinner?" I remember her asking Gretchen one night in the late seventies.

"Because we broke up a month ago and I've been in my room crying ever since?"

"Well, he still needs to *eat*," my mother said.

The fellow who wound up living in a city park—Kevin, I'll call him—started dropping by in the early eighties. His parents and mine owned some rental property together, and over the years both he and I performed odd jobs there. I remembered him as directionless and guessed from what my sister told me that he pretty much stayed that way. Still, it seemed incredible to me that something like this could happen, for we were middle-class and I'd been raised to believe that our social status inoculated us against severe misfortune. A person might be *broke* from time to time—who wasn't?—but you could never be poor the way that *actual* poor people were: poor with lice and missing teeth. Your genes would reject it. Slip too far beneath the surface, and wouldn't your family resuscitate you with a loan or rehab or whatever it was you needed to get back on your feet? Then there'd be friends, hopefully ones who went to college and might at the very least view you as a project, the thing they'd renovate after the kitchen was finished.

At what point had I realized that class couldn't save you, that addiction or mental illness didn't care whether you'd taken piano lessons or spent a summer in Europe? Which drunk or junkie or unmedicated schizophrenic was I crossing the street to avoid when I put it all together? I didn't know what the story was with Kevin. The two of us had had every advantage, yet now he was living in a thicket three miles from the house he grew up in.

My siblings and I used to worry that once our father was gone a similar fate might befall our sister Tiffany, who had committed suicide six months earlier. Like all of us, she received an inheritance a few years after our mother died. It wasn't a fortune, but it was certainly more than I had ever seen. The money arrived just after I really needed it, at a moment when, for the first time in my adult life, I was finally on my feet. I paid off my student loan with a portion of it. My father wanted me to invest the rest, but I didn't want the *idea* of money, I wanted the real thing, so I parked it in my checking account and would go to an ATM sometimes twice a day just to look at my balance on the screen. A year earlier the most I'd had was a hundred dollars. Now this.

It was interesting to see what we all did with our

inheritance. Pragmatic Lisa put her check in the bank. Gretchen moved south and saw to some bills while Amy and Paul essentially spent their money on candy. Tiffany was the only one who quit her job, thinking, I guess, that she was set. Within two years she was broke, but rather than rejoining the workforce, she decided that money was evil, as were most of the people who had it. She canceled her checking account and started bartering, exchanging a day's work for a carton of cigarettes or a bag of groceries. At night she'd go through people's trash cans, looking for things she could sell. It's like she saw poverty as an accomplishment. "I'll be out at one in the morning, knee-deep in a Dumpster and elbowing aside some immigrant Haitian lady for the good stuff," she boasted once when I visited her in Somerville.

"Maybe the Haitian woman *has* to be there," I said. "She has nothing at her disposal, while you have an education. You had braces on your teeth. You speak good English." My argument was an old and stodgy one: the best thing you can do for the poor is avoid joining their ranks, thus competing with them for limited goods and services.

On that same visit Tiffany explained that poor people refuse to answer surveys. "When census takers come to our doors, we ignore them." She spoke the way a tribal leader might to a visiting anthropologist. "We Pawnees grind our corn with a rock!"

Every time I visited, her apartment was more of a wreck, not just messy but filthy. "How can you live like this?" I asked the last time I was there.

"We poor people don't have the energy to clean up after ourselves," she told me.

After she was evicted, she lived in a series of single rooms, with people just as badly off as herself. According to Tiffany, the only thing wrong with her was her back—that's why at the age of forty-three she went on disability, she said. Since when, though, do they prescribe lithium and Klonopin for back pain? If she'd been more forthright, we could have put her behavior in context, could have said, when she tested our patience, "That's her illness talking." As it was, it didn't add up. "Why can't a grown woman hold a job?" we wondered. "Why does she have so many restraining orders against people?"

Tiffany would have inherited money from our father someday, though she likely would have burned right through it. "You want a car?" she'd have said, perhaps to someone she met in a parking lot. "I'll buy you a fucking Bronco or whatever. Is that what you want?"

Word would have gotten out that some lady was buying people Broncos, and in no time she'd have been penniless again and feeling just fine about it.

An hour before arriving at the beach, Hugh stopped at a fast-food place called Hardee's so I could get a coffee. The town we were in was small and grim, and the restaurant was deserted except for us. Inside the front door stood a Christmas tree, over-decorated in a majestic combination of red and gold. "How long has this been up?" I asked the black woman behind the counter.

She scratched at the tattoos on her left forearm, initials that looked like they'd been done at home with a sewing needle. "Since last Tuesday maybe?" She turned to the fellow cleaning the grill. "Do that sound right?"

"Just about," he said.

"Will you have a tree at home?" I asked. "Have you put it up yet?"

This is the sort of thing that drives Hugh crazy—*What does it matter if her Christmas tree is up?*—but there was no one in line behind me, and I was genuinely curious.

"I think it's too early," the woman said. "My kids is all excited for one, but we ain't even had Thanksgiving yet."

Gretchen ran her good hand over the false hair on top of her head. "Will you cook a turkey on Thursday or go for something else?"

"Are you two happy now?" Hugh asked when we finally returned to the car. "Need to go back in and learn what everyone's doing for New Year's, or do you think we can leave?"

Gretchen propped up her broken arm on the narrow window ledge. "If he thinks *we're* bad, he should spend more time with Lisa."

"That's true," I agreed. "Lisa's the master. I left her at a Starbucks for ninety seconds last year, and when I returned the woman behind the counter was saying to her, 'My gynecologist told me that exact same thing.'"

I normally don't believe in drinking coffee in the car. Most often, I spill more than I swallow, but without it I'd have fallen asleep and then had to revive myself once we reached the house. It was after eleven when we arrived, and I was pleasantly surprised by all the changes. The place we bought is two stories tall and divided down the middle into equal-size units. You can pass back and forth between one half and the other by way of a hotel-style connecting door in the living room, but it's inconvenient if you're upstairs. The two kitchens are another problem, as we really only need one. Our initial idea was to knock down some walls and transform it into a single six-bedroom home. Then I recalled our last trip to the beach and the number of times I found my brother lying on the sofa with his shoes on, and decided that two separate halves was probably a good idea. The left side, which was softly lit and decorated with carefully chosen midcentury furniture, was mine and Hugh's, while the junky right side was for everyone else. Of course other people could stay in our half, but only when we were there to monitor and scold them.

Because everyone was coming for Thanksgiving, the house was going to be full. The family was arriving in dribs and drabs, so for the first night it was just the three of us. On the second day, late in the afternoon, Lisa pulled up. I helped her unload her car, and then we took a walk on the beach. It was cold enough to see our breath, and a strong wind was blowing. "Did I tell you I got Tiffany's toxicology report?" she asked a while after we'd left the house. "They also sent me her death certificate, and apparently—"

At that moment a Labrador retriever bounded up, tail

wagging, a middle-aged woman in a baseball cap trotting behind it. "Brandy, *no*," she scolded, adding as she unfurled her leash, "I'm sorry."

"For what?" Lisa gathered the dog's head in her hands. "You're beautiful, aren't you?" she trilled in the melodic voice she uses for things with tails. "Yes, you are, and you know it." She turned to the owner. "How old is she?"

"Two years this February," the woman said.

"I have one that age," Lisa told her. "And she's a real handful."

I have no patience for this kind of talk and turned to face the ocean, waiting for the conversation to end. Hopefully then I could learn what our sister had used to kill herself with. We figured she had taken pills—Klonopin, most likely—and though it technically didn't matter if she'd mixed it with other things, we still wanted to know.

Behind me, Lisa was telling the strange woman that the Newfoundland water dog she had before the one she has now died after swallowing all her husband Bob's high blood pressure medication.

"My God," the woman said. "That must have been awful!"

"Oh, it was," Lisa told her. "We just felt so guilty."

The woman with the Labrador wished us a happy Thanksgiving, and as she headed down the beach, Lisa continued her story. "So they sent me the death certificate, and the cause isn't listed as a drug overdose but as asphyxiation."

"I don't get it," I said.

She sniffed her hands for dog and then stuffed them into

her coat pockets. "After taking the Klonopin, Tiffany put a plastic bag over her head." Lisa paused a moment to let that sink in. "I wrote to the state trooper who found her body and sent him a picture of her in her twenties, the pretty one we ran with her obituary. I just wanted him to know she was more than what he walked in on."

I've always liked to think that before killing myself I'd take the time to really mess with people. By this I mean that I'd leave them things, and write letters, nice ones, apologizing for my actions and reassuring them that there was nothing they could have said or done to change my mind. In the fantasy I'd leave money to those who'd have never expected it. *Who's he?* they'd wonder after opening the envelope. It might be a Polish lifeguard at the pool I used to go to in London, or a cashier I was quietly fond of. Only lately do I realize how ridiculous this is. When you're in the state that my sister was in, and that most people are in when they take their own lives, you're not thinking of anything beyond your own pain. Thus the plastic bag—the maximizer, as it were—the thing a person reaches for after their first attempt at an overdose fails and they wake up sick a day later thinking, *I can't even kill myself right.*

It's hard to find a bag without writing on it—the name of a store, most often. LOWE'S, it might read. SAFEWAY. TRUE VALUE. Does a person go through a number of them before making a selection, or, as I suspect, will any bag do, regardless of the ironic statement it might make? This is what was going through my mind when Lisa stopped walking and turned to me, asking, "Will you do me a favor?"

"Anything," I said, just so grateful to have her alive and beside me.

She held out her foot. "Will you tie my shoe?"

"Well ... sure," I said. "But can you tell me why?"

She sighed. "My pants are tight and I don't feel like bending over."

I knelt down into the damp sand and did as she'd asked. It was almost dark, and as I stood back up, I looked at the long line of houses stretching to the pier. One of them belonged to us, but I couldn't have begun to guess which one it was. Judging by distance was no help either, as I had no idea how long we'd been walking. Lisa hadn't spent any more time at the Sea Section than I had, so she wasn't much help. "Does our place have one deck or two?" she asked.

"Two?" I said. "Unless it has only one?"

The houses before us were far from identical. They were painted every color you could think of, yet in the weak light, reduced to basic shapes, their resemblance was striking. All were wooden, with prominent picture windows. All had staircases leading to the beach, and all had the air of a second home, one devoted to leisure rather than struggle. They likely didn't contain many file cabinets, but if you were after puzzles or golf clubs or board games, you'd come to the right place. The people in the houses looked similar as well. We could see them in their kitchens and family rooms, watching TV or standing before open refrigerators. They were white, for the most part, and conservative, the sort of people we'd grown up with at the country club, the kind

61

who'd have sat in the front of the plane and laughed when the man across the aisle compared his broken overhead bin to Obamacare. That said, we could have knocked on any of these doors, explained our situation, and received help. "These folks have a house but don't know which one it is!" I could imagine a homeowner shouting over his shoulder into the next room. "Remember when that happened to us?"

It's silly, but after a while I started to panic, thinking, I guess, that we could die out there. In the cold. Looking for one of my houses. I was just condemning Lisa for not bringing her phone when I spotted the broken fishing rod tied to our railing. I'd noticed it earlier that day and had made a mental note to remove it. "Paul put it there so he'd be able to tell which house was ours," Gretchen had told me.

I'd said, "Well, we'll see about *that*." Now here I was, seeing about it.

Hugh was in the kitchen on our side of the house, making soup, when we walked in. "We got lost!" Lisa told him. "Were you worried about us?"

He dried his hands on his apron and tried to pretend he'd known we were out. "Was I ever!" The air smelled pleasantly of chicken stock and onions. On the radio it was announced that the president would be pardoning a turkey and that its name was Popcorn.

"That's nice," Lisa said.

While she went to her room to change, I walked through the connecting door and into the second kitchen. There I found Gretchen standing at the counter before a bowl of sliced apples.

"Did Lisa by any chance tell you about Tiffany?" I asked. "The plastic bag, you mean?" Gretchen nodded. "She told me on the phone last week. I try not to think of it, but it's pretty much all I *can* think about. Our own sister, ending up that way."

I walked to the window and looked at the sky, which had now gone from bruise-colored to black. "Someone told me," I said, "that in Japan, if you commit suicide by throwing yourself in front of a train, your family gets fined the equivalent of eighty thousand dollars for all the inconvenience you caused." From behind me, I could hear Gretchen slicing more apples. "Of course," I continued, "if your family was the whole reason you were killing yourself, I suppose it would just be an added incentive."

Out on the beach I could see the beam of a flashlight skittering across the sand. Someone was walking past the house, maybe to their own place, or perhaps to one that they were renting for the long holiday weekend. If it was smaller than the Sea Section, or less well positioned, they maybe looked up into our gaily lit windows and resented us, wondering, as we often did ourselves these days, what we had done to deserve all this.

The Perfect Fit

I'm not sure how it is in small families, but in large ones relationships tend to shift over time. You might be best friends with one brother or sister, then two years later it might be someone else. Then it's likely to change again, and again after that. It doesn't mean that you've fallen out with the person you used to be closest to but that you've merged into someone else's lane, or had him or her merge into yours. Trios form, then morph into quartets before splitting into teams of two. The beauty of it is that it's always changing.

Twice in 2014, I went to Tokyo with my sister Amy. I'd been seven times already, so was able to lead her to all the best places, by which I mean stores. When we returned in January 2016, it made sense to bring our sister Gretchen with us. Hugh was there as well, and while he's a definite presence, he didn't figure into the family dynamic. Mates, to my sisters and me, are seen mainly as shadows of the people they're involved with. They move. They're visible in direct sunlight. But because they don't have access to our emotional buttons—because they can't make us twelve again, or five, and screaming—they don't really count as players.

Normally in Tokyo we rent an apartment and stay for a week. This time, though, we got a whole house. The neighborhood it was in—Ebisu—is home to one of our favorite shops, Kapital. The clothes they sell are new but appear to have been previously worn, perhaps by someone who was shot or stabbed and then thrown off a boat. Everything looks as if it has been pulled from the evidence rack at a murder trial. I don't know how they do it. Most distressed clothing seems obviously fake, but not theirs, for some reason. Do they put it in a dryer with broken glass and rusty steak knives? Do they drag it behind a tank over a still-smoldering battlefield? How do they get the cuts and stains so ... right?

If I had to use one word to describe Kapital's clothing, I'd be torn between "wrong" and "tragic." A shirt might look normal enough until you try it on and discover that the armholes have been moved and are no longer level with your shoulders, like a capital "T," but further down your torso, like a lowercase one.

Jackets with patches on them might senselessly bunch at your left hip, or maybe they poof out at the small of your back, where for no good reason there's a pocket. I've yet to see a pair of Kapital trousers with a single leg hole, but that doesn't mean the designers haven't already done it. Their motto seems to be "Why not?"

Most people would answer, "I'll tell you why not!" But I like Kapital's philosophy. I like their clothing as well, though I can't say that it always likes me in return. I'm not narrow enough in the chest for most of the jackets, but what was to stop me, on this most recent trip, from buying a flannel shirt made of five differently patterned flannel shirts ripped apart and then stitched together into a kind of doleful Frankentop? I got hats as well, three of them, which I like to wear stacked up, all at the same time, partly just to get it over with but mainly because I think they look good as a tower.

I draw the line at clothing with writing on it, but numbers don't bother me, so I also bought a tattered long-sleeved T-shirt with "99" cut from white fabric and stitched onto the front before being half burned off. It's as though a football team's plane had gone down and this was all that was left. Finally, I bought what might be called a tunic, made of denim and patched at the neck with defeated scraps of corduroy. When buttoned, the front flares out, making me look like I have a potbelly. These are clothes that absolutely refuse to flatter you, that go out of their way to insult you, really, and still my sisters and I can't get enough.

There are three Kapital stores in Ebisu, and their interior design is as off-putting as their merchandise. Most clothing hangs from the ceiling, though there are a few beat-up racks, and horizontal surfaces that items are strewn across. At one of the shops, the window display consisted of three carved penises arranged from small to large. The most modest was on par with a Coleman thermos, while the king-size one was as long and thick as a wrestler's forearm. Amy's eyes popped out of her head, and before I could stop her, she hoisted the middle one out of the window, crying, "Oh my goodness, it's teak! I thought from out on the sidewalk that it was mahogany!" As if she were a wood expert and saw nothing beyond the grain.

The salesman blinked as Amy turned the dildo upside down. Then she positioned her right hand at the base of the testicles and pretended she was a waitress. "Would anyone care for some freshly ground pepper?"

There are three other branches of Kapital in Tokyo, and we visited them all, and stayed in each one until our finger-prints were on everything. "My God," Gretchen said, trying on a hat that seemed to have been modeled after a used toilet brush and adding it to her pile, "this place is amazing. I had no idea!"

The main reason we asked Gretchen to join us is that she understands shopping. That is to say, she understands there is nothing *but* shopping—unlike our brother Paul or our sister Lisa, whose disinterest in buying things is downright masculine. She and her husband, Bob, don't exchange Christmas gifts but will, rather, "go in" on something: a new set of shelves for the laundry room, for instance, or a dehumidifier. They usually buy whatever it is in midsummer, so by December it's been forgotten. It's the same with their anniversary and birthdays: nothing. "But you can change that," I often tell her. "Right," she says, the way I do when someone suggests I learn how to drive.

And it's not just big-ticket items. She and I were at O'Hare Airport one afternoon and passed a place that sold nuts. "Why don't you get some for Bob?" I asked. "They would be a nice little something to bring him as a gift."

She looked at the stand, a cart, really, and frowned. "I would, but his dentist told him he has brittle teeth."

"He doesn't have to crack them open in his mouth," I said. "Everything here is preshelled."

"That's OK."

I would never leave town and not bring Hugh back a gift. Nor would he do that to me, though in truth I had to train him. He's normally not that much of a shopper, but Tokyo seems to knock something loose in him. Perhaps it's because it's so far away. The difference is that he's ashamed of it. I think it's something he gets from his mother, who considers shopping to be wasteful, or, worse still in her book, "unserious."

"Why go to a store when you could go to a museum?" she might ask.

"Um, because the museum doesn't sell shit?" My sisters and I refuse to feel bad about shopping. And why should we? Obviously we have some hole we're trying to fill, but doesn't everyone? And isn't filling it with berets the size of toilet-seat covers, if not more practical, then at least *healthier* than filling it with frosting or heroin or unsafe sex with strangers?

"Besides," Amy said at the dinner table on the first night of our vacation, "it's not like everything we buy is for ourselves. I'll be getting birthday presents for friends and all sorts of things for my godson."

"You don't have to convince me," I told her, as we're cut from the same cloth. Shopping has nothing to do with money. If you have it, you go to stores and galleries, and if not, you haunt flea markets or Goodwills. Never, though, do you *not* do it, choosing instead to visit a park or a temple or some cultural institution where they don't sell things. Our sister-in-law, Kathy, swears by eBay, but I like the social aspect of shopping, the getting out. The touching things and talking to people. I work at home, so most days the only contact I have, except for Hugh, is with salespeople and cashiers.

My problem is that if someone really engages me, or goes the slightest bit out of his way, I feel I have to buy whatever it is he's selling. Especially if it involves a ladder or a set of keys. That explains the small painting of a forsaken shack I bought on the fourth day of our vacation, at a place I like called On Sundays. It's on an odd-shaped scrap of plywood, and though it's by a contemporary artist I've always gotten a kick out of—an American named Barry McGee—and was probably a very fair price, I bought it mainly because the store manager unlocked the case that it was in.

"I would have got it if you hadn't," Amy, my enabler, said,

as I left with the painting in a recently purchased, very pricey tote bag that had cowboys on it.

Then it was on to another one of our favorite places, the Tokyo outpost of the Dover Street Market. The original store, in London, sells both clothing and the kind of objects you might find in a natural history museum. I got the inner ear of a whale there a few years back and a four-horned antelope skull that was found in India in 1890.

The Ginza branch sticks to clothing and accessories. I'd gone with Amy on our first trip together, in 2014, and left with a pair of wide-legged Paul Harnden trousers that come up to my nipples. The button-down fly is a foot long, and when I root around in my pockets for change, my forearms disappear all the way to the elbows. You can't belt something that reaches that high up on your torso, thus the suspenders, which came with the trousers and are beautiful, but still, suspenders! Clown pants is what they are—artfully hand-stitched, lined all the way to the ankle—but clown pants all the same. They cost as much as a MacBook Air, and I'd have walked away from them were it not for Amy saying, "Are you kidding? You *have* to get those."

This time I bought a pair of blue-and-white-polka-dot culottes. Hugh hates this sort of thing and accuses me of transitioning.

"They're just shorts," I tell him. "Bell-bottom shorts, but shorts all the same. How is that *womanly?*"

A year and a half earlier, at this same Dover Street Market,

I bought a pair of heavy black culottes. Dress culottes, you could call them, made by Comme des Garçons and also beautifully lined. They made a pleasant whooshing sound as I ran up the stairs of my house, searching in vain for whatever shoes a grown man might wear with them. Hugh disapproved, but again I thought I looked great, much better than I do in regular trousers. "My calves are my one good feature," I reminded him as he gritted his teeth. "Why can't I highlight them every now and then?" The dress culottes weren't as expensive as the pants that come up to my nipples, but still they were extravagant. I buy a lot of what I think of as "at-home clothes," things I'd wear at my desk or when lying around at night after a bath, but never outdoors. These troubling, Jiminy Cricket–style trousers, for instance, that I bought at another of my favorite Japanese stores, 45rpm. They have horizontal stripes and make my ass look like a half dozen coins collected in a sack made from an old prison uniform.

I'd have felt like a fool paying all that money and limiting my nipple-high pants and black dress culottes to home, so I started wearing them onstage, which still left me feeling like a fool but a different kind of one.

"I hate to tell you," a woman said after a show one night, "but those culottes look terrible on you."

I was shattered. "Really?"

"They're way too long," she told me.

And so I had them shortened. Then shortened again, at which point they no longer made the pleasant whooshing sound and were ruined.

"Are these too long for me?" I asked the saleswoman on our most recent trip.

"Not at all," I'm pretty sure she told me.

A few days later, at the big Comme des Garçons shop in Omotesandō, I bought yet another pair of culottes, a fancier pair that are cerulean blue. "What are you *doing?*" Hugh moaned as I stepped out of the dressing room. "That's *three pairs* of culottes you'll own now."

All I could say in my defense was "Maybe I have a busy life."

I then tried on a button-down shirt that was made to be worn backward. The front was plain and almost suggested a straitjacket. You'd have to have someone close you into it and, of course, knot your tie if you were going for a more formal look. I'd have bought it were it not too tight at the neck.

"Maybe it'll fit after you have your Adam's apple shaved off," Hugh said.

Amy loaded up at Comme des Garçons as well, buying, among other things, a skirt that looks to have been made from the insides of suit pockets.

"What just happened?" she asked as we left the store, considerably more broke, and went up a few doors to Yohji Yamamoto, where I bought what Hugh calls a dress but what is most certainly a smock. A denim one that has side pockets. The front closes with snaps and, for whatever reason, the back does as well.

Most days we returned to our rental house groaning beneath the weight of our purchases, things I'd often wind up regretting the moment I pulled them out of their bags: a pair of drawstring jeans two sizes too large, for instance— drawstring jeans!—or a wool shirt that was relatively sober and would have been great were I able to wear wool. As it is, it causes me to itch and sweat something awful. "Then why did you get it?" Hugh asked. "Because everyone else got something," I told him, adding that it was on sale and I could always send it to my father, who might not wear it but would undoubtedly appreciate the gesture.

Shopping with my sisters in Japan was like being in a pie-eating contest, only with stuff. We often felt sick. Dazed. Bloated. Vulgar. Yet never quite ashamed. "I think I need to lie down," I said one evening. "Maybe with that brand-new eighty-dollar washcloth on my forehead."

Nothing was a total waste, I reasoned, as paying for it gave me a chance to practice my Japanese.

"I am buying something now," I'd say as I approached the register. "I have money! I have coins too!"

As if he or she had been handed a script, the cashier would ask where I was from and what I was doing in Tokyo.

"I am American," I would say. "But now I live in England. I am on vacation with my sisters."

"Oh, your sisters!"

Then I started saying, "I am a doctor."

"What kind?" asked a woman who sold me a bandanna with pictures of fruit and people having sex on it.

"A ... children's doctor," I said.

I wouldn't set out to misrepresent myself, but I didn't

know the word for "author" or "trash collector." "Doctor," though, was in one of the ninety "Teach Yourself Japanese" lessons I'd reviewed before leaving England.

I loved the respect being a pediatrician brought me in Japan, even when I wore a smock and had a tower of three hats on my head. You could see it in people's faces. I grew before their very eyes.

"Did you just tell that lady you're a doctor?" Amy would ask. "A little," I'd say.

A week after leaving Tokyo, I was on a flight from Hobart, Tasmania, to Melbourne, and when a passenger got sick and the flight attendant asked if there was a physician on board, my hand was halfway to the call button before I remembered that I am not, in fact, a doctor. That I just play one in Japan.

Though it cut into our shopping time, one thing we all looked forward to in Tokyo was lunch, which was always eaten out, usually at some place we'd just chanced upon. One afternoon toward the end of our vacation, settling into my seat at a tempura restaurant in Shibuya, I looked across the table at Amy, who was wearing a varsity sweater from Kapital that appeared to have bloodstains and bits of brain on it, and at Gretchen, with her toilet-brush hat. I was debuting a shirt that fell three inches below my knees. It was black and made me look like a hand puppet. We don't have the same eyes or noses, my sisters and I. Our hairlines are different, and the shapes of our faces, but on this particular afternoon the family resemblance was striking. Anyone could tell that we were related, even someone from another planet who believed that humans were as indistinguishable from one another as acorns. At this particular moment of our lives, no one belonged together more than us.

Who would have thought, when we were children, that the three of us would wind up here, in Japan of all places, dressed so expensively like mental patients and getting along so well together? It's a thought we all had several times a day: *Look how our lives turned out! What a surprise!*

When the menus came, Gretchen examined hers upside down. She had never used chopsticks before coming to Tokyo, and for the first few days she employed them separately, one in each hand, like daggers. Amy was a little better, but when it came to things like rice she tended to give up and just stare at her bowl helplessly. Always, when the food was delivered, we'd take a moment to admire it, so beautifully presented, all this whatever it was: The little box with a round thing in it. The shredded bit. The flat part. Once, we ate in what I'm pretty sure was someone's garage. The owner served only one thing, and we had it seated around a folding table, just us and a space heater. The food was unfailingly good, but what made lunch such a consistent pleasure was the anticipation, knowing that we had the entire afternoon ahead of us and that it might result in anything: Styrofoam boots, a suit made of tape—whatever we could imagine was out there, waiting to be discovered. All we Sedarises had to do was venture forth and claim it.

Leviathan

As I grow older, I find that the people I know become crazy in one of two ways. The first is animal crazy—more specifically, dog crazy. They're the ones who, when asked if they have children, are likely to answer, "A black Lab and a sheltie-beagle mix named Tuckahoe." Then they add—they always add—"They were rescues!"

The second way people go crazy is with their diet. My brother, Paul, for instance, has all but given up solid food, and at age forty-six eats much the way he did when he was nine months old. His nickname used to be the Rooster. Now we call him the Juicester. Everything goes into his Omega J8006—kale, carrots, celery, some kind of powder scraped off the knuckles of bees—and it all comes out dung-colored and the texture of applesauce. He's also taken to hanging upside down with a neti pot in his nose. "It's for my sinuses," he claims.

Then there's all his disease prevention, the things that supposedly stave it off but that the drug companies don't want you knowing about. I've heard this sort of thing from a number of people over the years. "Cancer can *definitely* be cured with a vegan diet," a friend will insist, "only *they* want to keep it a secret." In this case the "they" that doesn't want you to know is the meat industry, or "Big Meat."

"If a vegan diet truly did cure cancer, don't you think it would have at least made the front page of the *New York Times* Science section?" I ask. "Isn't that a paper's job, to tell you the things 'they' don't want you to know?"

Paul insists that apricot seeds prevent cancer but that the cancer industry—Big Cancer—wants to suppress this information, and has quietly imprisoned those who have tried to enlighten us. He orders in bulk and brought a jarful to our house at the beach one late May afternoon. They're horribly bitter, these things, and leave a definite aftertaste. "Jesus, that's rough," my father said after mistaking one for an almond. "How many do you have in a day?"

Paul said four. Any more could be dangerous, since they have cyanide in them. Then he juiced what I think was a tennis ball mixed with beets and four-leaf clovers.

"Add some strawberries and I'll have a glass as well," my sister Lisa said. She's not convinced about the cancer prevention but is intrigued by all the weight our brother has lost. When he got married in 2001, he was close to 200 pounds—which is a lot if you're only five foot two. Now he was down to 135. It's odd seeing him thin again after all these years. I expected him to look the way he did when he was twenty, before he ballooned up, and while he's the same physical size as he was back then, his face has aged and he now looks like that kid's father. It's as if a generation of him went missing.

Part of Paul's weight loss can be attributed to his new liquid diet, but I think that exercise has more to do with it. He bought a complicated racing bike and rides it while wearing what looks like a Spider-Man costume and the type of cycling shoes that have cleats on them. One day that May, as I walked to the post office, he pedaled past without recognizing me. His face was unguarded, and I felt I was seeing him the way other people do, at least superficially: this boyish little man with an icicle of snot hanging off his nose. "Mornin'," he sang as he sped by.

It's ridiculous how often you have to say hello on Emerald Isle. Passing someone on the street is one thing, but you have to do it in stores as well, not just to the employees who greet you at the door but to your fellow shoppers in aisle three. Most of the houses that face the ocean are rented out during the high season, and from week to week the people in them come from all over the United States. Houses near the sound, on the other hand, are more commonly owner-occupied. They have landscaped yards, and many are fronted by novelty mailboxes. Some are shaped like fish, while others are outfitted in cozies that have various messages—BLESS YOUR HEART or SANDY FEET WELCOME!—printed on them.

The neighborhoods near the sound are so Southern that people will sometimes wave to you from *inside* their houses. Workmen, hammers in hand, shout hello from ladders and half-shingled roofs. I'm willing to bet that the local operating rooms are windowless and have doors that are solid wood. Otherwise the surgeons and nurses would feel obliged to acknowledge everyone who passed down the hall, and patients could possibly die as a result.

While the sound side of the island feels like an old-fashioned neighborhood, the ocean side is more like an upscale retirement community. Look out a street-facing window on any given morning, and you'd think they were filming a Centrum commercial. All these hale, silver-haired seniors walking or jogging or cycling past the house. Later in the day, when the heat cranks up, they purr by in golf carts, wearing visors, their noses streaked with sunblock. If you were a teenager, you likely wouldn't give it much thought, but to my sisters and me—people in our mid- to late fifties—it's chilling. *That'll be us in, like, eight years,* we think. *How can that be when only yesterday, on this very same beach, we were children?*

Of course, the alternative is worse. When my mother was the age that I am now, she couldn't walk more than ten steps without stopping to catch her breath. And stairs—forget it. In that regard, our father is her opposite. At ninety-one, the only things wrong with him are his toes. "My doctor wants to cut one off, but I think he's overreacting," he said on the second morning of our vacation. The sun shone brightly through the floor-to-ceiling windows, and he was sitting shirtless at the kitchen table on the side of the house that Hugh and I share, wearing black spandex shorts.

The toes he presented for my inspection looked like fingers playing the piano, all of them long and bent and splayed. "How do you fit those things into shoes?" I asked, wincing. "Wouldn't it be easier to go the Howard Hughes route and just wear tissue boxes on your feet?"

Just then, the plumber arrived to look at our broken dishwasher. Randy is huge in every way, and as we shook hands I thought of how small mine must have felt within his, like a paw almost. "So, what seems to be the problem?" he asked.

It's the same story every time: Hugh calls and schedules an appointment regarding something I know nothing about. Then he leaves for God knows where and I'm left to explain what I don't understand. "I guess it's not washing the dishes right, or something?" I said.

Randy pulled a screwdriver from his tool belt and bent down toward a panel. "I'd have come sooner, but we're still catching up from the winter we had. Pipes frozen, all kinds of mess."

"Was it that cold?" I asked.

"Never seen anything like it," he said.

My father raised his coffee cup. "And they talk about global warming. Ha!" After twenty minutes or so, Randy suggested we get a new dishwasher, a KitchenAid, if possible. "They're not that expensive, and it'll probably be cheaper than fixing this here one." I showed him to the door, and as he made his way down the stairs, my father asked when I was going to have my prostate checked. "You need to get that taken care of ASAP. While you're at it, you might want to get a complete physical. I mean, the works."

What does that have to do with the dishwasher? I wondered.

When Hugh returned, I passed on Randy's suggestion regarding the KitchenAid, and he nodded. "While he was here, did you ask him about the leak under the sink?"

"I didn't know I was supposed to."

"Goddamn it, I told you last night—"

My father tapped me on the shoulder. "You need to call a doctor and get a checkup."

This was my second trip to our house on Emerald Isle, and the second time my entire family, or what was left of it, was assembling here. Summer was still a month away, and already the temperature was in the nineties. The humidity was high, and once you left the beach the breeze disappeared, inviting in its dearth great squadrons of biting flies. Still, I would force myself out every afternoon. On one of my walks, I came across my brother and his daughter, Madelyn, standing on a footbridge a few blocks inland from our house and dropping bread into the brackish canal. I thought they were feeding fish, but it turned out they were throwing the food to turtles, dozens of them. Most had shells between six and eight inches long and are what my sister Gretchen, who owns a lot of reptiles, calls sliders. Then there were the snapping turtles. The largest measured around three and a half feet from nose to tail. Part of his left front foot was missing, and he had a tumor on his head the size of my niece's fist.

"And you're giving them *bread?*" I said to Paul. It made me think of my first visit to Spokane, Washington. I was walking through the park that fronts the river there and happened upon people feeding animals that resembled groundhogs.

"What are these?" I asked a man who was kneeling with his arm outstretched.

"Marmots," he told me. "And what do they eat?"

He reached into a bag he kept at his feet. "Marshmallows." I've subsequently seen people feed all sorts of things to the turtles in the canal on Emerald Isle: dry dog food, Cheerios, Pop-Tarts, potato chips.

"None of that is good for them," Gretchen says. Her turtles eat mainly worms and slugs. They like fruit as well, and certain vegetables. "But potato chips, no."

"What about *barbecue* potato chips?" I asked.

During the week that we spent at the beach, I'd visit the canal every afternoon, sometimes with raw hot dogs, sometimes with fish heads or chicken gizzards. The sliders would poke their heads out of the water, begging, but it was the snappers I was there for. Seeing one was like seeing a dinosaur, for isn't that what they are? Watching as they tore into their food, I'd shiver with fear and revulsion, the way I used to when watching my brother eat. On YouTube there's a video of one biting off a finger, and of the man whose finger it used to be acting terribly surprised, the way that people who offer sandwiches to bears, or jump security fences to pose beside tigers, ultimately are. There are other videos of snapping turtles eating rats and pigeons and frogs, all of which are still alive, their pathetic attempts at self-defense futile. It's a kind of pornography, and after sitting for twenty minutes, watching one poor animal after another being eviscerated, I erase my Internet user history, not wanting to be identified as the person who would find this sort of thing entertaining—yet clearly *being* that person.

Did it help, I wondered, that my favorite turtle was the one with the oversize tumor on his head and half of his front foot missing? Did that make me a friend of the sick and suffering, or just the kind of guy who wants both ice cream *and* whipped cream on his pie? Aren't snapping turtles terrible enough? Did I really need to supersize one with a cancerous growth?

My main reason for buying the house on Emerald Isle was that it would allow my family to spend more time together, especially now, while my father's still around. Instead, though, I was spending all my time with these turtles. Not that we didn't do anything as a group. One afternoon we scattered my mother's ashes in the surf behind the house. Afterward, standing on the shore with the empty bag in my hands, I noticed a trawler creeping across the horizon. It was after shrimp, or some kind of fish, and hovering over it, like flies around a garbage pail, were dozens of screaming sea-birds. It made me think of my mother and how we'd follow her even to the bathroom. "Can't I have *five minutes?*" she'd plead from behind the locked door as we jiggled the handle, relating something terribly important about tights, or a sub-stitute teacher, or a dream one of us had had about a talking glove. My mother died in 1991, yet reaching into the bag, touching her remains, essentially throwing her away, was devastating, even after all this time.

Later, drained, we piled into the car and drove to the small city of Beaufort. There we went to a coffee shop and fell in line behind a young man with a gun. It was tucked into a holster he wore belted around his waist, and after he had gotten his order and taken a seat with two people I took to be his parents, we glared at him with what might as well have been a single eye. Even my father, who laughs appreciatively at such bumper stickers as DON'T BLAME ME, I VOTED FOR THE AMERICAN, draws the line at carrying a pistol into a place where lattes are being served. "What's he trying to prove?" he asked. The guy was my height or maybe a little shorter, wearing pressed jeans. "He's obviously got a complex of some kind," my sister-in-law, Kathy, said.

"It's called being a Republican," Lisa offered.

My father frowned into his decaf. "Aw, come on, now."

I mentioned a couple of T-shirts I'd seen people wearing on the pier not far from my turtle spot. INVEST IN HEAVY

METALS, read one, and it pictured three bullets labeled BRASS, COPPER, and LEAD. Another showed a pistol above the message WHEN YOU COME FOR MINE, YOU BETTER BRING YOURS.

"Since when is the government coming for anyone's guns in this country?" I asked. "I mean, honestly, can't any of us enter a Walmart right now and walk out with a Sidewinder missile?"

It was a nice moment, all of us on the same page. Then my father ruined it by asking when I'd last had a physical.

"Just recently," I said. "Recently, like when?"

"1987," I told him, adding, after he moaned, "You *do* know this is the fourth time today you've asked me about this, right? I mean, you're not just being ninety-one, are you?"

"No," he said. "I know what I'm saying."

"Well, can you please *stop* saying it?"

"I will when you get a physical."

"Is this really how you want to be remembered?" I asked. "As a nagger ... with hammertoes?"

"I'm just showing my concern," he said. "Can't you see that I'm doing this for your own good? Jesus, son, I want you to have a long, healthy life! I love you. Is that a crime?"

The Sea Section came completely furnished, and the first thing we did after getting the keys was to load up all the televisions and donate them to a thrift shop. It's nice at night to work puzzles or play board games or just hang out, maybe listening to music. The only one this is difficult for is my father. Back in Raleigh, he has two or three TVs going at the same time, all tuned to the same conservative cable station, filling his falling-down house with outrage. The one reprieve is his daily visit to the gym, where he takes part in a spinning class. Amy and I like to joke that his stationary bike has a front wheel as tall as a man and a rear one no bigger than a pie tin—that it's a penny-farthing, the kind people rode in the 1880s. On its handlebars we imagine a trumpet horn with a big rubber bulb on one end.

Being at the beach is a drag for our father. To his credit, though, he never complains about it, just as he never mentions the dozens of aches and pains a person his age must surely be burdened by. "I'm fine just hanging out," he says. "Being together, that's all I need." He no longer swims or golfs or fishes off the pier. We banned his right-wing radio shows, so all that's left is to shuffle from one side of the house to the other, sometimes barefoot and sometimes wearing leather slippers the color of a new baseball mitt.

"Those are beautiful," I said the first time I noticed them. "Where did they come from?"

He looked down at his feet and cleared his throat. "A catalog. They arrived back in the early eighties, but I only just recently started wearing them."

"If anything should ever ... happen to you, do you think that maybe *I* could have them?" I asked.

"What would ever happen to me?"

In the ocean that afternoon, I watched my brother play with his daughter. The waves were high, and as Madelyn hung laughing off Paul's shoulders, I thought of how we used to do the same with our own father. It was the only time any of us ever touched him. Perhaps for that reason I can still recall the feel of his skin, slick with suntan oil and much softer than I had imagined it. Our mother couldn't keep our hands off her. If we'd had ink on our fingers, at the end of an average day she'd have been black, the way we mauled and poked and petted her. With him, though, we never dared get too close. Even in the ocean, there'd come a moment when, without warning, he'd suddenly reach his limit and shake us off, growling, "God almighty, will you just leave me alone?"

He was so much heavier back then, always determined to lose thirty pounds. Half a century later he'd do well to *gain* thirty pounds. Paul embraced him after our sister Tiffany died and reported that it was like hugging a coatrack. "What I do," he says every night while Hugh puts dinner together, "is take a chicken breast, broil it with a little EVOO, and serve it with some lentils—*fan*tastic!" Though my father talks big, we suspect the bulk of his meals come from whatever they're offering as free samples at his neighborhood Whole Foods, the one we give him gift cards for. How else to explain how he puts it away while we're all together, eating as if in preparation for a fast?

"Outstanding," he says between bites, the muscles of his jaws twitching beneath his spotted skin. "My compliments to the chef!"

One night, I looked over and saw that he was wearing a

Cherokee headdress someone had brought to the house for Thanksgiving. Paul had put it on him and, rather than shake it off the way he would have a few years earlier, he accepted it—owned it, really. Just before dessert was served, Amy and I noticed that he was crying. He looked like the Indian from that old "Keep America Beautiful" ad campaign. One single tear running down his cheek. He never blubbered or called attention to himself, so we never asked what the problem was, or if there even *was* a problem. "Maybe he was happy that we were all together," Lisa said when we told her about it. Gretchen guessed that he was thinking about our mother, or Tiffany, while Paul wondered if it wasn't an allergic reaction to feathers.

It's not that our father waited till this late in the game to win our hearts. It's that he's succeeding.

"But he didn't *used* to be this nice and agreeable," I complained to Hugh.

"Well, he is now," he said. "Why can't you let people change?"

This is akin to another of his often asked questions: "Why do you choose to remember the negative rather than the positive?"

"I don't," I insist, thinking, *I will never forget your giving me such a hard time over this.*

Honestly, though, does choice even come into it? Is it my fault that the good times fade to nothing while the bad ones burn forever bright? Memory aside, the negative just makes for a better story: the plane was delayed, an infection set in, outlaws arrived and reduced the schoolhouse to ashes. Happiness is harder to put into words. It's also harder to source, much more mysterious than anger or sorrow, which come to me promptly, whenever I summon them, and remain long after I've begged them to leave.

For whatever reason, I was very happy with my snapping turtles. In the wild, they can live for up to thirty years, though I fear that my favorite, the one with the hideous growth on his head, might not make it that long. There's something wrong with his breathing, though he still manages to mount the females every chance he gets.

"Oh, look," a passerby said, pointing down into the churning water on the last full day of our vacation. "They're playing!"

I looked at the man with an incredulity that bordered on anger. "Snapping turtles don't *play*," I said. "Not even when they're babies. They're reptiles, for Christ's sake."

"Can you believe it?" I said to my father when I got back to the beach house that evening. He was standing beside the sofa, wearing a shirt I clearly remember throwing into his trash can in the summer of 1990, and enjoying a glass of vodka with a little water in it. All around him, people were helping with dinner. Lisa and Amy were setting the table while Gretchen prepared the salad and Paul loaded his juicer with what looked like dirt. Hugh brought fish up from the grill, and as Kathy and Madelyn rounded up chairs, I put on some music. "Attaboy," my father said. "That's just what we needed. Is this Hank Mobley?"

"It is," I told him.

"I thought so. I used to have this on reel-to-reel tape."
While I know I can't control it, what I ultimately hope to
recall about my late-in-life father is not his nagging or his
toes but, rather, his fingers, and the way he snaps them when
listening to jazz. He's done it forever, signifying, much as a
cat does by purring, that you may approach. That all is right
with the world. "Man, oh man," he'll say in my memory, lift-
ing his glass and taking us all in, "isn't this just *fan*tastic?"

Your English Is So Good

There's a language instruction course I turn to quite often. Pimsleur, it's called, and I first used it in 2006, when preparing for a trip to Japan. "I am American," I was taught to announce, somewhat sheepishly, at the start of lesson one. Half an hour later, I'd advanced to 日本語がお上手ですね, which translates to "Your Japanese is so good!"

It seemed a bit early in the game to be receiving compliments, but still I learned to recognize the phrase and to respond to it with りがとうございます、ですが私はまだそんなに上手ではありません ("Thank you very much, but I am not really skilled yet"). This came in handy as, once I got to Tokyo, every time I opened my mouth I was clobbered with praise, even if I was just saying something simple like "Huh?"

The same was true with a number of other phrases I'd considered unnecessary but heard again and again once I arrived in Japan. The fact is that, unless we're with friends or family, we're all like talking dolls, endlessly repeating the same trite and tiresome lines: "Hello, how are you?" "Hot enough out there?" "Don't work too hard!"

I'm often misunderstood at my supermarket in Sussex, not because of my accent but because I tend to deviate from the script.

Cashier: Hello, how are you this evening?
Me: Has your house ever been burgled?
Cashier: What?
Me: Your house—has anyone ever broken into it and stolen things?

With me, people aren't thinking *What did you say?* so much as *Why are you saying that?*

I know that Pimsleur offers an English course for native Spanish speakers, but I'm not sure if it's geared toward U.K. English or what you hear in the United States. The former would most certainly include "At the end of the day ..." Turn on British TV or follow anyone named Ian for more than a few minutes, and you're guaranteed to hear it. In France the most often used word is *"connerie,"* which means "bullshit," and in America it's hands-down "awesome," which has replaced "incredible," "good," and even "just OK." Pretty much everything that isn't terrible is awesome

94

in America now. Pimsleur has made me hyperaware of the phrases I hear most often over the course of an average day, so aware that I've started jotting them down in hopes of putting together my own English program, one for business travelers visiting the United States. Let's start at the airport newsstand, shall we? There, you'll lay a magazine upon the counter and be asked by the cashier, "Do you need some water to go with that?" This will be said as if the two things should not really be sold separately, as if in order to properly read a copy of *Us Weekly* you'll have to first rinse your eyes out with a four-dollar bottle of Evian.

The practice of pushing more stuff on you is called "upselling" and is one of those things that, once you notice it, you can't *stop* noticing. At the airport in Baton Rouge a few years back, I ordered a coffee.

"Do you need a pastry to go with that?" the young man behind the counter asked.

"I wasn't too shy to order the coffee," I said, "so what makes you think I'd hold back on a bear claw if I wanted one?"

The fellow shrugged. "We have Danish too."

This made me furious. "On second thought, I don't want anything," I told him. Then I went a few doors down to Dunkin' Donuts and said, "I would like nothing but coffee. Just coffee. Period."

The woman behind the counter crossed her arms. "No cup?"

"Well, of course I want a cup."

"No milk or nothing?"

This always happens when I try to make a point. "And milk," I told her. "Coffee in a cup with some milk in it but nothing else." Then, of course, my flight got delayed by two hours and I had to go crawling back for some Munchkins. "Do you need coffee or a soda to go with that?" the woman who'd replaced the one I spoke to earlier asked.

Increasingly at Southern airports, instead of a "good-bye" or "thank-you," cashiers are apt to say, "Have a blessed day." This can make you feel like you've been sprayed against your will with God cologne. "Get it off me!" I always want to scream. "Quick, before I start wearing ties with short-sleeved shirts!"

As a business traveler, you'll likely be met at your destination by someone who asks, "So, how was your flight?" This, as if there are interesting variations and you might answer, "The live orchestra was a nice touch," or "The first half was great, but then they let a baby take over the controls and it got all bumpy." In fact, there are only two kinds of flights: ones in which you die and ones in which you do not.

Next you'll meet the desk clerk at your hotel, a woman most likely, in her mid- to late thirties. She won't know if you've driven to this city or flown and will ask after taking your credit card, "So how was your trip in?"

There's really no answer but "Fine." I mean, there is, but I'm guessing she won't want to hear it. *Or would she?*

Her: So how was your trip in?

You: Well, I was originally going to fly, but then this tiger offered to carry me very gently in her mouth. I said OK, but you know what? She wasn't gentle at all. One of her teeth pierced my small intestine, so now, on top of everything else, I have to shit in a bag every day for the rest of my life!

Her: Well, that is just awesome. We're all so glad you made it.

After the desk clerk hands you your key, the bellman will grab your suitcase and ask, "So where are you coming in from today?" Like everyone else at the hotel, he doesn't really listen to your answer. His words are just a hook to hang a tip on. You could say you're from a town ten miles down the road or from another dimension. Either way, you get the same response: "You're a long way from home, aren't you?"

I object to these questions, not because they're personal but because they're *not*. "Instead of asking how my trip in was, why not ask ... I don't know ... if I have a godson?" I said to a desk clerk not long ago.

She took off her glasses and rubbed the bridge of her nose. "All right, do you have a godson?"

"I do," I said. "He's eight years old and is named Tommy. How about you? Do you have any godchildren?"

"No," the woman told me. "I have not had that pleasure." She smiled like someone who'd learned to do so in a book, and I realized that if I wanted to make contact I needed to dig a little deeper. "He has cancer," I said.

The desk clerk put her hand over her heart. "Oh, poor thing!"

"That's OK," I sighed. "I'm sure that within a year or two someone else will ask me to be a godfather."

It wasn't true that Tommy had cancer.I just wanted to get a rise out of her, to feel some kind of pulse. I knew that the young woman had a life. She'd gone to school somewhere. She had friends. I didn't need a fifteen-minute conversation, just some human interaction. It can be had, and easily: a gesture, a joke, something that says, "I live in this world too." I think of it as a switch that turns someone from a profession to a person, and it works both ways. "I'm not just a vehicle for my wallet!" I sometimes want to scream.

Go to a restaurant anywhere in the United States, and three minutes after your food is delivered, your server will return to the table, asking, "How's that Southeastern Lard Pocket?" Once, in Kansas City, this was amended to "How's that Southeastern Lard Pocket tasting for you?" As if the lard pocket had the tongue instead of me.

"Mmmm," I said, my mouth full the way it always is when the server returns.

"Awesome," I was told. "I hope you're saving some room for dessert." This, with the chuckle that means "Wouldn't it be funny if what I just said was funny?"

The following morning you'll wander to the hotel breakfast room and tell the hostess that there is only one in your party. She'll pick up a menu and lead you to your table, asking, "And how is your day going so far?"

"You mean the last twelve minutes?" you'll ask. "OK, I guess."

And she'll say, "Awesome."

If you've come directly downstairs, this might be the first time since last night that you've heard this word. That doesn't make it refreshing. Rather, it's like being in Alaska and getting bitten by your first blackfly of the day. *I am going to be bleeding by sunset,* you'll think.

More often than not, your breakfast room will have a TV in it, tuned to a twenty-four-hour cable-news network. Sometimes you'll see two TVs or more. At a place I stayed at in Kentucky one year, there were eight. After I ordered, the waitress went around with her remote and activated each one, making me think of a lamplighter, if lamps were instruments of torture rather than things that make it easier for you to see how old and tired-looking you've gotten. "People like it," she said when I asked if it was really necessary at six o'clock in the morning.

You hear this a lot in America, especially when you're complaining about televisions, or loud music, or, more common still, television *and* loud music together in the same room. "People like it."

"Yes," I always want to say, "but they're the *wrong* people."

On leaving your hotel, you'll likely be offered a bottle of water, and urgently, by the fellow who just brought your car around. "You'll need this for your trip to the airport."

"I'm actually not *walking* there," I always say. "This car is taking me, and I should arrive in no time."

Everyone in America is extremely concerned with hydration. Go more than five minutes without drinking, and you'll surely be discovered behind a potted plant, dried out like some escaped hermit crab. When I was young no one would think to bring a bottle of water into a classroom. I don't think they even sold bottled water. We survived shopping trips without it, and funerals. Now, though, you see people with those barrels that Saint Bernards carry around their necks in cartoons, lugging them into the mall and the movie theater, then hogging the fountains in order to refill them. *Is that really necessary?* I think as I stand behind them with an aspirin dissolving in my mouth, fuming.

Should you wander into a shop during your visit to the United States, you can expect a clerk to ask, "So what are we up to today?" "We," as if the two of you had made plans you forgot about.

"Oh," I usually say, already sorry I walked in, "I'm just looking around."

"Awesome."

If you purchase something, you'll be asked at the register what you're going to do with the rest of your afternoon.

"Umm, I don't know. Buy more shit?"

My friend Ronnie manages a shoe store, so is fluent in this kind of talk. When we're out together, she takes over, and effortlessly, while I look on, amazed. "Doing about as well as can be expected," she says when asked about her health by someone who could not possibly give a fuck. Because she lives in California, Ronnie is on the front lines.

"Did you catch that?" she whispered one afternoon in San Francisco. "That salesman just said, 'Welcome in.'"

"So?" I asked.

"That's the latest thing," she told me. "I'm hearing it everywhere now."

"Should we add it to the list?"

"Definitely."

"The list" is a growing collection of words and phrases we'd outlaw if given the power to do so. It includes "awesome," of course, and "It is what it is," which is ubiquitous now and means absolutely nothing, as far as we can see.

"Isn't that the state motto of South Dakota?" I said the second or third time I heard it.

Some of my additions to the list were things that Ronnie wasn't familiar with. "We're all going to the same place," for instance. This is what novice fliers in group five say when they get caught trying to board with group two. Sure, we're all headed to St. Louis. The difference is that some people (me) are going to find room in the overhead bins and others (you) are not.

These same passengers can be counted on to catch my eye and moan, "Hurry up and wait," when traffic backs up on the Jetway.

I cock my head and look at them with an expression that translates to *Why is stuff coming from that hole in your face?*

*

Another word I've added to "the list" is "conversation," as in "We need to have a national conversation about_____." This is employed by the left to mean "You need to listen to me use the word 'diversity' for an hour." The right employs obnoxious terms as well—"libtard," "snowflake," etc.—but because they can be applied to me personally it seems baby-ish to ban them.

I've outlawed "meds," "bestie," "bucket list," "dysfunc-tional," "expat," "cab-sav," and the verb "do" when used in a restaurant, as in "I'll do the snails on cinnamon toast."

"Ugh," Ronnie agrees. "Do!—that's the worst."

"My new thing," I told her, "is to look at the menu and say, 'I'd like to purchase the veal chop.'"

A lot of our outlawed terms were invented by black people and then picked up by whites, who held on to them way past their expiration date. "My bad," for example, and "I've got your back" and "You go, girlfriend." They're the verbal equiv-alents of sitcom grandmothers high-fiving one another, and on hearing them, I wince and feel ashamed of my entire race.

The weak link of my American English for Business Travelers program is the "business" part. It used to be that I could eavesdrop on a conversation and learn that the two men at the next table were doctors, or that one was a massage ther-apist and the other sold life insurance for cats. Now, though, I have no idea what anyone does, especially if the people I'm listening in on are under forty. I hear the words "integration" and "platform" a lot, but not in any recognizable context.

Theirs are the offices, I imagine, where Kayson rides his scooter down the concrete hallway, passing a warren of workspaces that resemble cages. And no one's shirt is tucked in. That's one phrase that won't be in my English book: "Nice suit." Twenty years from now they probably won't be making them anymore. Dressing up will mean wearing the sweatpants without paint on them to your father's funeral.

My *American English for Business Travelers* will teach you to recognize the most often repeated words and phrases but hopefully leave room for wonder. I'm constantly surprised and delighted by some of the things I hear while traveling across the United States. I'm thinking of a fellow bus passenger who turned to me as our driver barely missed a pedestrian, saying, "See, he don't love life." Of a Memphis panhandler who called as I passed, "Hey, man, why don't you buy me a Co-Cola?" Of the newsstand cashier who did not suggest I buy a bottle of water but, rather, looked at the price of my *Sunday Times* and said, "That's five dollars, baby. You OK widdat?" Or of the pilot who somberly said as he turned off the seat belt sign at the end of a flight, "All rise."

Now *that's* what I'm talking about.

Calypso

The deal with America is that it's always something. I go twice a year and arrive each time on the heels of a major news story: SARS, anthrax, H1N1. Bedbugs! In the fall of 2014 the story was Ebola, not the thousands who had died of it in Africa but the single person who had it in Dallas. Because there are TVs everywhere one goes—restaurants; hotel lobbies; airports, even, I discovered; doctors' waiting rooms—and because they're all tuned to one cable-news network or other, the coverage was inescapable. Every angle was explored, then subsequently beaten to death. When the patient, whose name was Thomas Duncan, died, you'd think he'd taken half the country down with him. A teacher in Maine was sent home because she'd flown to Dallas, not to the hospital where the man had been cared for but just to the city. Schools closed. Hysterical parents were interviewed. "Ebola is here," we were told by the media, "and it's coming to get you."

I started seeing people wearing face masks in the airport and decided that I hated them. What bugged me, I realized, was their flagrant regard for their own lives. It seemed not just overcautious but downright conceited. I mean, why should *they* live?

"Stay safe," a Starbucks employee said to me one morning. I was in a hurry to get to my gate, so didn't stop to ask, "Safe from what?"

I was in the United States for a lecture tour: forty-five cities in forty-seven days. "My God!" people say when they look at my schedule. But it isn't like *real* work. The travel can occasionally be taxing, but anyone can turn pages and read out loud. What takes time are the postshow book signings—my fault because I talk too much. "What kind of a name is *Draven?*" I asked one evening, squinting at the Post-it Note attached to the title page.

"I don't know exactly," the woman on the other side of the table said. "He's a friend of my brother."

I looked at the name again. "Draven. It sounds like . . . the past-past tense of 'drove.'"

In most of the cities on my tour I didn't know anyone, but here and there I caught up with people. In Winston-Salem it was my sister Lisa. A week later in Omaha I saw my old friend Janet and her twenty-five-year-old son, Jimmy, who is tall and thin and was sporting a long rust-colored beard. Back when we met in the late 1980s, Janet was highlighting the grain in rectangular sheets of plywood. That was her artwork. Now she just leaves the rectangles as they are and has founded something called the Wood Interpretation Society. "Jimmy," she said, standing in the living room that doubles as her studio, "fetch me my stick."

Her son handed her a length of bamboo, and she used it to point to her most recent piece. "All right, can you see the snowman?"

I saw nothing, so she gestured to two knots. "His eyes. You can't see his eyes?"

"Well, OK," I said. "Sure ... a little."

"And now can you see that he's talking to an owl?"

"Owls are a dime a dozen in woodgrain," Jimmy explained. "That's true," his mother said, and she moved on to her next piece of plywood, in which a turtle considered a mountain. "And this is all just found!" she told me. "I honestly haven't altered a thing!"

Later, over coffee, we got onto the subject of elderly parents. Janet's mother is eighty-nine and is in excellent physical and mental health. "Unlike my friend Phil's mother," she said. "This was a woman who never missed a church service, who was an absolute pillar of her community. Then she got dementia and became a different person." She poured me more coffee. "The last time Phil saw her, she leaned over in her wheelchair and at the top of her voice said, 'Hitler wants my pussy.'"

Jimmy stroked his biblike beard. "They say he was quite the ladies' man."

"Who even knew that word was in her vocabulary?" Janet asked. "And *how* had Hitler told her? He'd been dead for fifty years by that point."

Being with Janet reminded me of how lucky I am. At ninety-two, my father is in great shape. And should that suddenly change for any reason, he probably won't linger all that long. I'd like to think I inherited his constitution, but in fact I'm more like my mother. Thus I took it seriously when, at the postshow book signing that night in Omaha, a fellow with a noticeable divot in his face pointed to a dark spot beside my left eye, saying, "I'm no doctor, but am ninety percent sure you have skin cancer."

Four days later I saw a dermatologist in Jackson Hole, Wyoming. The spot, he said, was nothing to worry about. Then he used the word "cancer," albeit with a "pre-" in front of it—"a little *precancerous* keratosis." He hit it with some liquid nitrogen, and by the time I left his office it looked like I had a pencil eraser stuck to my face. The following day on the plane, the eraser burst and precancer juice ran like a fat tear down my cheek.

That was the first of several procedures I wound up having over the course of my tour. Funny, but for years I avoided going to any kind of doctor. If it was an emergency, I could be talked into it, but anything else, especially anything preventative, was out of the question. Then my father forced me to get a colonoscopy, and a whole new world opened up. The paperwork is a drag, of course, so many forms that by the time you're in the examining room you have to add "carpal tunnel" to your already long list of complaints. As far as the doctors themselves go, though, I've had a pretty good run. In the summer of 2014, while on vacation at my family's beach house on the coast of North Carolina, and again at the insistence of my father, I went in for a physical. "All right, then," the GP said, after taking my blood pressure and looking into my ears, "what do you say you stand up now and I'll do your front and back."

It was such a classy, understated way to say, "After grabbing your balls I'd like to stick my finger up your ass."

The dermatologist was fun to talk to, as was a nurse who gave me a flu shot while I was passing through O'Hare. The only exception I've had so far is a surgeon I saw on the coast of North Carolina a few days after having my physical. Six years earlier, I had noticed a lump on my right side, just at the base of my rib cage. It was, I later learned, a lipoma, meaning a harmless fatty tumor. It continued to grow for the next several months until it was the size and feel of an unshelled hard-boiled egg. I could have lived with it for the rest of my life, but after spending some time along the canals not far from our beach house, I got a better idea. The surgeon I met with didn't have much in the way of a personality. That's not to say he was rude, just perfunctory. He took an ultrasound of my fatty tumor and said that he could remove it the following week.

"Terrific," I said, "because I want to feed it to a snapping turtle."

"Excuse me?"

"Not just *any* snapping turtle," I continued, as if that was what had given him pause. "There's one very *specific* turtle I'm planning to feed it to. He has a big growth on his head."

"It's against federal law for me to give you anything I've removed from your body," the surgeon said.

"But it's *my* tumor," I reminded him. "*I* made it."

"It's against federal law for me to give you anything I've removed from your body."

"Well, could I maybe have *half* to feed to this turtle?"

"It's against federal law for me to give you anything I've removed from your body."

I left with my tumor intact, thinking, *Honestly. What has this country come to?*

On tour sometimes, just before the question-and-answer part of the evening, I'll stand at the podium and run my mouth for a while. I told the story about the tumor onstage in El Paso, Texas, and afterward a woman approached my signing table, saying, "I'll cut that out of you tonight if you like. *And* I'll let you keep it."

I pointed out the long line, and she shrugged. "No problem, I'm a night owl." She handed me a slip of paper with her number on it. "Just phone me when you're done."

The woman looked to be around fifty, Mexican, I reckoned, and as short as a child. "In case you're wondering, I *am* a doctor," she said. "Not a surgeon, but I studied it for a year in med school, and unless your tumor has its own blood supply, removing it should be fairly easy."

Its own blood supply! I thought of those people you read about sometimes with terrible potato-size twins inside of them, complete with hair and teeth. Recounting this story over the next few weeks, I was surprised by the general reaction it got. "She *what?* You didn't take her up on it, did you?"

"Well, sure."

"And how did you know that she was a *real* doctor?"

These were the same overly cautious people who threw out their children's Halloween candy and showed up at airports with masks on. "How do I know she was a doctor? She told me she was."

The only real exception was my father, who once took antibiotics prescribed for his dog, saying, "Aw, who cares? They're the same damn thing." When I told him that a strange woman performed surgery on me in the middle of the night, his response was the same as mine would have been: "Sounds like you saved yourself some real money!"

The doctor—I'll call her Ada—returned to the theater after I'd finished signing books, at around one a.m. With her were the son and daughter of her girlfriend, both of whom were in their early thirties and looked more like soap-opera actors than real people. While their attractiveness was preternatural—almost outlandish—the way they related to each other as brother and sister felt familiar to me, especially their little insults, blanks, for the most part, more funny than mean. The four of us drove on deserted roads across the state line to a dark clinic located in what seemed like the middle of nowhere. The late hour, the secrecy—it felt furtive and dangerous, like having an abortion in 1950.

My procedure began with a local anesthetic, and though I didn't notice when Ada cut into me, I could feel slight tugs as she hacked at the tumor. It was like having my pocket picked by a trainee. My fatty pocket. The shreds were placed in a metal pan and resembled slivers of raw chicken breast.

"Are my intestines hanging out?" I asked at one point. "God, no," Ada said. "Your lipoma is in a sort of pouch, so there's nothing at all protruding from the incision. If you want, you can look for yourself. I can get you a mirror."

"That's OK," I said.

While she worked, I talked to the son and daughter of her girlfriend, hyperconscious of how good they looked and, by contrast, how awful I did, half sitting up, my hairy stomach showing. "How do you say 'tumor' in español?" I asked.

"Tumor," the woman said.

I took Spanish in high school and am always delighted when I find another word I can toss into my vocabulary basket. It was like learning that shortcake is pronounced "shorto cakey" in Japanese, and beige "beige" in German.

After I was stitched back up, we drove to Ada's house, the only one with lights burning on its quiet suburban street. There I met her girlfriend, Anna, who wore a floor-length white nightgown. Her hair was white as well and fell to the middle of her back. "So nice of you to drop by," she said, opening a bottle of codeine tablets. "Will you take some for the road? For the pain?"

The house felt familiar, if not exactly like the one I grew up in, then at least close. "Artsy," my mom would have called it, meaning there were paintings on the walls but they weren't all pretty. The backyard was flooded with moonlight, and while looking out at the sleeping city below us, Anna's daughter told me about her youngest child, a girl of five. "She's going through a phase where she wants to be a dog, *insists* she's a dog. The barking and walking on all fours is something I'm willing to put up with, but then she shit on the ground over by that shrub, and I said, 'That's it. Now you've gone too far.'"

At four a.m. Ada and her girlfriend's children returned me to my hotel, and three hours later I got up to go to the airport. All told, it was an exceptional evening: a chance to meet interesting new people and have at least one of them reach inside of me with her tiny hands. After I left El Paso, Ada shipped my tumor on ice to my sister's house in Winston-Salem. Lisa put it in the freezer and promised to bring it with her to the beach when we gathered for Thanksgiving at the end of my tour.

Meanwhile I continued on. In Houston I had an emergency root canal, which didn't hurt nearly as much as I thought it would. A few days later, perhaps because hanging out with doctors was something I'd gotten into the habit of,

I saw a podiatrist in Dallas. "What seems to be the problem?" he asked.

"My left foot hurts," I told him.

He took some X-rays, but nothing showed up, perhaps because my foot only hurt a little.

"This has to stop," said my lecture agent, who'd been making all the appointments for me and was clearly tired of it.

My last show was in Tallahassee, Florida, and the following morning I flew to Raleigh. My sister Gretchen picked me up at the airport, and by sunset we were with Hugh and my entire family at the house on Emerald Isle. I like having a place that theoretically belongs to everyone but technically belongs to me. It's neutral ground but not quite, meaning that if someone hangs a picture I don't care for, I get to take it down, saying, "Let's rethink this." I, on the other hand, can hang whatever I like. "Why would anyone frame a piece of plywood?" my father asked the night before Thanksgiving.

He was frowning at the artwork Janet had given me during my visit to Omaha. "It's a one-eyed raccoon looking in a mirror," I told him.

He took his glasses off and rubbed his eyes. "Like hell it is." This Thanksgiving my brother-in-law, Bob, was deep-frying the turkey. It has to be done outdoors, so while he scoped out a spot and constructed a wind barrier, I took my frozen tumor and headed to the canal with Lisa and my niece, who was eleven years old at the time and very shy.

It was cold, and during the fifteen-minute walk, I asked Madelyn who the most popular girl at her school was.

She answered with no hesitation. "And is she nice?" I asked.

"She wasn't last year or the year before, but she is now."

"You will never forget the name of the most popular girl in the sixth grade," I said. "Even when you're old and on your deathbed it'll come to you. That is her triumph."

"My most popular girl was Jane-Jane Teague," Lisa told us.

"That's such a good name," I said.

Lisa nodded. "And you had to call her Jane-Jane—even the teachers. She wouldn't answer to anything less."

We arrived at the canal to find three boys standing on the footbridge and looking down into the water, their bikes sprawled like bodies on the ground around them. I leaned over the rail, but instead of the snapping turtles I was expecting, I saw only sliders, which are significantly smaller and less awe-inspiring.

"You looking for Granddaddy?" the boy beside me asked. I said, "Granddaddy?"

"People call him Godzilla sometimes too," the kid told me. "He's the one with the messed-up head. Me and my brother feed him toast a lot."

"And grapes," the boy next to him said. "We give him them and crackers if we got 'em."

I felt betrayed, the way you do when you discover that your cat has a secret secondary life and is being fed by neighbors who call him something stupid like Calypso. Worse is that he loves them as much as he loves you, which is to say

115

not at all, really. The entire relationship has been your own invention.

"I never knew the turtle had a name," I said. The kid shrugged. "Sure does."

"So where is he now?"

"Hibernating," the boy told me. "Like every year." I was crestfallen. "And when will he wake up?"

The kid reached down and picked up his bike. "Springtime, 'less he dies in his sleep. What, you bring some bread for him?"

"Me?" I said. "No." Ashamed to admit it was something more intimate.

"And after everything I went through!" I whined on our way back to the house.

"Your lipoma will keep," Lisa assured me. "We'll just put it back in the freezer and you can feed it to Godzilla or Granddaddy or whatever his name is when you return in May."

"And what if there's a storm between now and the spring, and the electricity goes out?"

Lisa thought for a moment. "Something that's going to eat a tumor probably won't distinguish between a good one and a bad one."

I won't say the hibernating turtle ruined my Thanksgiving. He *did* make it feel rather anticlimactic, though I'm not sure why. If you were to throw a lipoma to a dog, he'd swallow it in a single bite, then get that very particular look on his face that translates to *Fuck. Was that a tumor?* There'd be something to see. Turtles, on the other hand, never change expression and live with fewer regrets. I'm certain that when I return in May and drop my little gift into the canal, the snapper will eat it unthinkingly, the way he's eaten all the chicken hearts and fish heads I've thrown to him over the past year. Then he'll look around for more before disappearing, like the ingrate that he is, back into his foul and riled depths.

A Modest Proposal

London is five hours ahead of Washington, DC, except when it comes to gay marriage. In that case, it's two years and five hours ahead, which was news to me. "Really?" I said, on meeting two lesbian wives from Wolverhampton. "You can do that here?"

"Well, *of course* they can," Hugh said when I told him about it. "Where have you been?"

Hugh can tell you everything about the current political situation in the U.K. He knows who the chancellor of the exchequer is, and was all caught up in the latest election for the whatever-you-call-it, that king-type person who's like the president but isn't.

"*Prime minister?*" he said. "Jesus. You've been here *how* long?"

It was the same when we lived in Paris. Hugh regularly read the French papers. He listened to political shows on the radio, while I was, like, "Is he the same emperor we had last year?"

When it comes to American politics, our roles are reversed. "What do you mean 'Who's Claire McCaskill?'" I'll say, amazed that I—that *anyone,* for that matter—could have such an ignorant boyfriend.

I knew that the Supreme Court ruling on gay marriage was expected at ten a.m. on June 26, which is three p.m. in Sussex. I'm usually out then, on my litter patrol, so I made it a point to bring my iPad with me. When the time came, I was standing by the side of the road, collecting trash with my grabber. It's generally the same crap over and over—potato-chip bags, candy wrappers, Red Bull cans—but along this particular stretch, six months earlier, I'd come across a strap-on penis. It seemed pretty old and was Band-Aid colored, about three inches long and not much bigger around than a Vienna sausage, which was interesting to me. You'd think that if someone wanted a sex toy she'd go for the gold, sizewise. But this was just the bare minimum, like getting AAA breast implants. Who had this person been hoping to satisfy, her Cabbage Patch doll? I thought about taking the penis home and mailing it to one of my sisters for Christmas but knew that the moment I put it in my knapsack, I'd get hit by a car and killed. That's just my luck. Medics would come and scrape me off the pavement, then, later, at the hospital, they'd rifle through my pack and record its contents: four garbage bags, some wet wipes, two flashlights, and a strap-on penis.

"There must be some mistake," Hugh would tell them. "You said it was *how* big?"

My iPad could get no signal at three p.m., so I continued walking and picking up trash, thinking that, whichever way the Supreme Court went, I never expected to see this day in my lifetime. When I was young, in the early seventies, being gay felt like the worst thing that could happen to a person, at least in Raleigh, North Carolina. There was a rumor that it could be cured by psychiatrists, so for most of my teens that's where I placed my hope. I figured that eventually I'd tell my mother and let her take the appropriate steps. What would kill me would be seeing the disappointment on her face. With my father I was used to it. That was the expression he naturally assumed when looking at me. Her, though! Once when I was in high school she caught me doing something or other, imitating my Spanish teacher, perhaps with a pair of tights on my head, and said, like someone at the end of her rope, "What are you, *a queer?*"

I'd been called a sissy before, not by her but by plenty of other people. That was different, though, as the word was less potent, something used by children. When my mother called me a queer, my face turned scarlet and I exploded. "*Me?* What are you talking about? Why would you even *say* a thing like that?"

Then I ran down to my room, which was spotless,

everything just so, the Gustav Klimt posters on the walls, the cornflower-blue vase I'd bought with the money I earned babysitting. The veil had been lifted, and now I saw this for what it was: the lair of a blatant homosexual.

That would have been as good a time as any to say, "Yes, you're right. Get me some help!" But I was still hoping that it might be a phase, that I'd wake up the next day and be normal. In the best of times, it seemed like such a short leap. I *did* fantasize about having a girlfriend—never the sex part, but the rest of it I had down. I knew what she'd look like and how she'd hold her long hair back from the flame when bending over a lit candle. I imagined us getting married the summer after I graduated from college, and then I imagined her drowning off the coast of North Carolina during one of my family's vacations. Everyone needed to be there so they could see just how devastated I was. I could actually make myself cry by picturing it: How I'd carry her out of the water, how my feet would sink into the sand owing to the extra weight. I'd try mouth-to-mouth resuscitation, and keep trying until someone, my father most often, would pull me back, saying, "It's too late, son. Can't you see she's gone?"

It seemed I wanted to marry just so I could be a widower. So profound would be my grief that I'd never look at another woman again. It was perfect, really. Oh, there were variations. Sometimes she'd die of leukemia, as in the movie *Love Story*. Occasionally a madman's bullet would fell her during a hostage situation, but always I'd be at her side, trying everything in my power to bring her back.

The fantasy remained active until I was twenty. Funny how unimportant being gay became once I told somebody. All I had to do was open up to my best friend, and when she accepted it I saw that I could as well.

"I just don't see why you have to rub everyone's noses in it," certain people would complain when I told them. Not that I wore it on T-shirts or anything. Rather, I'd just say "boyfriend" the way they said "wife" or "girlfriend" or "better half." I insisted that it was no different, and in time, at least in the circles I ran in, it became no different.

While I often dreamed of making a life with another man, I never extended the fantasy to marriage or even to civil partnerships, which became legal in France in 1999, shortly after Hugh and I moved to Paris. We'd been together for eight years by that point, and though I didn't want to break up or look for anyone else, I didn't need the government to validate my relationship. I felt the same way when a handful of American states legalized same-sex marriage, only more so: I didn't need a government *or* a church giving me its blessing. The whole thing felt like a step down to me. From the dawn of time, the one irrefutably good thing about gay men and lesbians was that we didn't force people to sit through our weddings. Even the most ardent of homophobes had to hand us that. We were the ones who toiled behind the scenes while straight people got married: the photographers and bakers and florists, working like Negro porters settling spoiled passengers into the whites-only section of the train.

"Oh, Christopher," a bride might sigh as her dressmaker zipped her up, "what would I have ever done without you?"

What saved this from being tragic was that they were doing something we wouldn't dream of: guilt-tripping friends and relatives into giving up their weekends so they could sit on hard church pews or folding chairs in August, listening as the couple mewled vows at each other, watching as they were force-fed cake, standing on the sidelines, bored and sweating, as the pair danced, misty-eyed, to a Foreigner song.

The battle for gay marriage was, in essence, the fight to be as square as straight people, to say things like "My husband tells me that the new Spicy Chipotle Burger they've got at Bennigan's is awesome!"

That said, I was all for the struggle, mainly because it so irritated the fundamentalists. I wanted gay people to get the right to marry, and then I wanted none of us to act on it. I wanted it to be ours to spit on. Instead, much to my disappointment, we seem to be all over it.

I finally got a signal at the post office in the neighboring village. I'd gone to mail a set of keys to a friend and, afterward, I went out front and pulled out my iPad. The touch of a finger and there it was, the headline story on the *New York Times* site: "Supreme Court Ruling Makes Same-Sex Marriage a Right Nationwide."

I read it and, probably like every American gay person, I was overcome with emotion. Standing on the sidewalk, dressed in rags with a litter picker pinioned between my legs, I felt my eyes tear up, and as my vision blurred I considered all the people who had fought against this and thought, *Take that, assholes.*

The Supreme Court ruling tells every gay fifteen-year-old living out in the middle of nowhere that he or she is as good as any other dope who wants to get married. To me it was a slightly mixed message, like saying we're all equally entitled to wear Dockers to the Olive Garden. Then I spoke to my accountant, who's as straight as they come, and he couldn't have been more excited. "For tax purposes, you and Hugh really need to act on this," he told me.

"But I don't want to," I said. "I don't believe in marriage."

He launched into a little speech, and here's the thing about legally defined couples: they save boatloads of money, especially when it comes to inheriting property. My accountant told me how much we had to gain, and I was, like, "Is there a waiting period? What documents do I need?"

That night, I proposed for the first of what eventually numbered eighteen times. "Listen," I said to Hugh over dinner, "we really need to do this. Otherwise when one of us dies, the other will be clobbered with taxes."

"I don't care," he told me. "It's just money."

This is a sentence that does not register on Greek ears. It's *just* a mango-size brain tumor. It's *just* the person I hired to smother you in your sleep. But since when is money *just* money?

"I'm not marrying you," he repeated.

I swore to him that I was not being romantic about it: "There'll be no rings, no ceremony, no celebration of any kind. We won't tell anyone but the accountant. Think of it as a financial contract, nothing more."

"No."

"Goddamn it," I said. "You are going to marry me whether you like it or not."

"No, I'm not."

"Oh, yes you are."

After two weeks of this, he slammed his fork on the table, saying, "I'll do anything just to shut you up." This is, I'm pretty sure, the closest I'm likely to get to a yes.

I took another ear of corn. "Fine, then. It's settled."

It wasn't until the following day that the reality set in. I was out on the side of a busy road with my litter picker, collecting the shreds of a paper coffee cup that had been run over by a lawn mower, when I thought of having to tick the box that says "married" instead of "single." I always thought there should have been another option, as for the past twenty-four years I've been happily neither. I would never introduce Hugh as my husband, nor would he refer to me that way, but I can easily imagine other people doing it. They'd be the type who so readily embraced "partner" when it came down the pike, in the mid-nineties. Well-meaning people. The kind who wear bike helmets. It occurred to me while standing there, cars whizzing by, that the day I marry is the day I'll get hit and killed, probably by some driver who's texting or, likelier still, sexting. "He is survived by his husband, Hugh Hamrick," the obituary will read, and before I'm even in my grave I'll be rolling over in it.

That night at dinner, neither of us mentioned the previous evening's conversation. We talked about this and that, our little projects, the lives of our neighbors, and then we retreated to different parts of the house—engaged, I suppose, our whole lives ahead of us.

The Silent Treatment

Aside from an occasional dinner party thrown by one of his neighbors, the only thing my father gets dressed up for anymore is church. When I was young he'd drop my sisters and me off in time for Sunday school, then head to the club to play golf and return at the end of the service, most often after everyone else had left and it was just us standing alone in front of the shuttered building. Now, though, he's there every week.

"In a suit?" I asked.

"Well, of course," he said. "What do you think?" It was late May and he was sitting on the deck at the Sea Section, looking out at the ocean, which was relatively calm that day and topaz-colored. Amy and Lisa were at the table too. Hugh had made us BLTs, and as he set them before us, my father rubbed his hands together. "*Fan*tastic!"

Even in his old age he's a good-looking man, skin still fairly taut, with an enviable, easy-to-draw nose, all straight line with no bumps. I'd love to have inherited it, but instead I resemble my mother—nostrils big enough to stuff olives into. He still has most of his hair, my father, some of it relatively dark. On this day it was covered by a flat-topped cap I'd bought him in London. It was made of cotton, with a bright pattern of small checks, and though when I gave it to him he claimed to hate it, he'd been wearing it since he arrived.

"Why do you want to know what I wear to church?" he asked.

I brought up a barbecue restaurant Hugh, Amy, and I had stopped at a few days earlier on our way from Raleigh to Emerald Isle. It was noon on Sunday in a small eastern North Carolina town. I figured that most everyone had come from church and found it interesting that the only men in jackets and ties were Mexican. "The rest of them had Dockers on and polo shirts," I said. "Women wore slacks as well."

"And?" my father asked.

"It's just something I noticed, that's all. When we were young, we had to get dressed up. Now I hear that people are wearing shorts to church and even sweatpants."

My father winced. "Well, not at the Holy Trinity."

Before our church moved in the 1980s, it was in a stone building located in downtown Raleigh. The neighborhood was thought of as rough, at least by suburbanites like us, and though nothing bad ever happened, occasionally something exciting did. "Say, Dad, remember the time you had a meeting with the priest and I went with you?" Lisa asked. "We were on our way back home when a black man exposed himself to us. I think I was twelve or thirteen, and he just pulled his penis right out of his pants and started waving it around."

"Oh, right." Our father wiped his mouth. "I remember that like it was yesterday!"

"Then you made a U-turn so we could see it again." He chuckled. "It was big!"

"Most fathers would shield their daughters from something like that," Lisa said. "But there *you* were, making sure I got a second look."

Again he laughed. "I guess I saw it as an educational experience!"

I like it when Lisa and Hugh are around, as they can always get my father to talk. When it's just the two of us, I never know what to say. This is hardly a new development. It's been like this for as long as I can remember.

All his life my father has been handy. He worked on his own cars and once built an addition onto our house in Raleigh. My job, always, was to hand him tools as he called for them and to hold the worklight, a bare bulb in an aluminum cage. It might have been different had I cared what a piston was, or were I interested in the proper consistency of cement. As it was, I never asked, and he never offered.

Rather, I'd just stand there, my arm outstretched like a lawn jockey's.

"Goddamn it, quit moving."

"I'm not."

"Well, you sure as hell are, so stop it."

I suppose I could have asked him questions about his job, or his childhood, but it already seemed too late to get into it. These were the sorts of conversations that should have begun years earlier. They needed foundations built brick by brick, and not just thwacked down whole. He could have asked about my life, but I don't know how articulate I would have been. "What were you thinking, slapping that beef roast with your bare hands?"

"I dunno."

I wasn't being cagey. I honestly hadn't a clue why I'd done it. The roast was on a serving tray, puddled in its own juices—juices that, when I hit it, spattered all over the pastel family portrait we'd sat for earlier that week at the mall. I watched the blood drip down our faces, and then I slapped the roast again, wondering all the while what had come over me. It was the same when I took an industrial stapler to our new kitchen countertops, an out-of-body experience.

What do other fathers and sons talk about? I'd ask myself, shifting the worklight from one hand to the other. There was never any problem making conversation with my mother. That was effortless, the topics springing from nowhere, and we'd move from one to the next in a way that made me think of a monkey gracefully swinging through the branches of a tree. The silence my father and I inflicted on each other back then is now exacerbated by his advanced age. Every time I see him could be the last, and the pressure I feel to make our conversation meaningful paralyzes me. "How do you talk to him so easily?" I asked Lisa as we carried the lunch dishes back into the house.

"It's simple," she told me. "Sometimes I'll just call and say, 'Hey, Dad, what are you up to?'"

"Watching Fox News while doing his taxes no matter what month it is or what time of day," I said.

"Well, yes, but maybe he found a new deduction. Maybe someone from church died, or one of his old neighbors. You never know!"

That night, we went to a restaurant Lisa and her husband, Bob, are fond of in the town of Atlantic Beach. I put on a shirt and tie, Amy debuted a new dress, and my father wore a T-shirt with white tennis shorts. His legs used to be hairy, but now they're as smooth as a child's, the result, he says, of wearing knee-high socks for all those years at IBM. He rode to the restaurant with Hugh and me, and perked up when, halfway through the twenty-minute drive, we passed the condominium complex we often stayed at in the 1980s. "Hey," he said, "that's where we used to go when we were a family."

"Well, aren't you still a family?" Hugh asked. "I meant when Sharon was alive."

Though I hated hearing him say that, I couldn't deny the

truth of it. Our mother was the one who held us all together. After her death we were like a fistful of damp soil, loose bits breaking off with no one to press them back in. When she was around, we came to the beach every year. The place we'd just passed was set in a complex of twenty or so units, arranged around a pool. There are pictures of us all standing on the deck, my eyes and those of several of my sisters blood-shot from all our pot-smoking. I think of the meth-fueled sandcastles we built and the dinosaurs made of driftwood the year we could afford cocaine.

"You're all bright-eyed and bushy-tailed," our mother used to say when we'd return from our midnight walks on the beach. She knew what was up, while I don't think our father had a clue. The condo we rented was arranged over five floors. When my sisters brought boyfriends, they had to sleep in separate rooms. It was the same at my parents' place in Raleigh. "It's my house, so you play by *my* rules," our mother used to say. The sole exception was me, for some reason. I said to my father not long ago, "The only sex you and Mom allowed under your roof was *gay* sex. Didn't that seem odd to you?"

"Well, there was *us*," he said. "Us?"

"I mean your mother and me."

I covered my ears and vomited a little in my mouth.

The restaurant in Atlantic Beach resembled a shack, so I was surprised by the fancy menu, which was handed out by a young, bow-lipped woman with a sweet eastern

North Carolina accent. "I like to start with the women if that's OK," she said when it came time to take our orders. She turned to Lisa. "So what will you be having this evening, milady?"

It was such an unexpected word, so refined, and Amy repeated it all night. "How were your five double Scotches, milady?" When our food arrived, I mentioned a flight attendant I'd recently met. "I was asking her about the things passengers leave behind on planes, and she told me that earlier that week she discovered a used Kotex in one of the seat backs."

"Oh my God," Amy said, delighted. "And it was still warm," I added.

My father looked down at his flounder. "Is that any way to talk at the table?"

"He's disgusting," Hugh said, happy to have found something he and my father could agree on.

I then brought up a fellow I'd met in New Mexico who has an uncle named Phil McCracken.

"What's wrong with that?" my father asked.

"Fill my crack in," Lisa said. "Get it? Like butt crack?"

My father sighed. "The level of discourse here is definitely lacking."

"So tell me, Lou," Hugh said, "what was *your* father like?" He was trying to open things up a bit and didn't realize that, subject-wise, he'd steered us onto a dead-end street. My grandfather, the man we addressed as Pappoú, died when I was six years old. He came from Greece, as did Yiayiá, my grandmother. Neither of them spoke more than a hundred words of English, yet they owned and ran a newsstand in Cortland, New York. The space was long and dim and narrow, like a hallway that led to nothing, lit by a bare bulb. They lived in the small apartment upstairs, and though I can picture it clearly, all I remember about Pappoú is that he was short—five foot one, according to his immigration papers. "Why are you asking about my father?" my father said. Hugh shrugged. "I've just never heard much about him." My father signaled the waitress for another vodka tonic.

"Well, he was a very ... hard worker."

"You're not going to get any more than that out of him," Lisa said to Hugh. "Believe me, we've been trying all our lives."

I never told my father,but a few years earlier I'd received a letter from an eighty-two-year-old woman in Cortland. She said some nice things about my books, then added, "Your grandfather was a pig." Then it was just her name, no "best wishes" or anything.

"I have nothing more to tell you," my father said when Hugh asked for details. "The man worked very hard, both my parents did. There wasn't time for anything else." It's maddening how tight-lipped he is on the subject. Greeks tend to disapprove when their children marry outside the culture, so Pappoú was a real dick to my mother. She'd shudder at the mention of his name but never got specific, saying only, "You'll have to take that up with your father."

"How can you not have a single memory of him?" I asked

later that night on our way home from the restaurant. "I mean, there has to be *something* you recall. Did he drive a car? Did he ever listen to music or read? I remember Yiayiá saying some pretty rough things about black people, which is odd given her limited vocabulary. It's like she took English lessons from a Klan member but quit after the second day. Was he that way too? Did he smoke? Did he give you Christmas presents?"

"He's asleep," Hugh told me.

"What?"

"Your dad, he's asleep."

The next morning I saw my father at the dining room table, leafing through a magazine Bob had brought. It was about North Carolina crafts and had a salad bowl on the cover. "Hey," he cried, looking up as I came down the stairs, "there he is!"

Lisa entered at around the same time, saying, "How you doing, Dad?"

"*Fan*tastic."

It is my habit to write in the morning, so I made a pot of coffee and carried it up to the room Hugh and I share. My worktable is in a corner, beside a sliding glass door that looks out onto the ocean, and I'd been sitting at it for an hour or so when my father wandered in. This is something he's done since I was a child. I'd be at my desk, drawing or doing homework, and he'd come in and stretch out on the bed.

"What's going on?" he'd ask.

A minute later he'd be fast asleep. This continued after I moved out and had my own apartment on the other side of Raleigh. He'd walk in without knocking and go straight to my bed, almost urgently, as if it were a toilet he desperately needed to use.

"So what's going on?" my father asked, hands on his hips, looking out my sliding glass door at the ocean.

"Nothing," I said. "Just trying to get some work done." He sat on the edge of the bed and tested it, the way you might if you were shopping for a new mattress. I noticed that his feet barely touched the floor, and as he lifted them in order to stretch out, I turned back to my computer and finished a letter I was writing to a convict. I get a lot of mail from people in prison, both men and women. They rarely say what they're in for, but what with the Internet, it's easy enough to find out—drugs, in this case.

"So how are you doing?" my father asked. "How's your health?"

This was possibly the tenth time in two days that he'd asked me this question. "Fine."

"You feeling pretty good?"

"I guess."

I can see him doing the same thing I am, trying to make some sort of connection. We're like a pair of bad trapeze artists, reaching for each other's hands and missing every time. Meanwhile the stage crew has gathered below us and begun to roll up the safety net.

"Thank you for dinner last night," my father said. "That was awfully generous of you."

"It was my pleasure." I returned my attention to the letter I was writing and wondered who might be the first to read it. Someone must surely open the envelopes before they get to the inmates, searching for money and easy-to-hide drugs. By the time I turned back to my father, he was snoring, which was for the best, probably.

Growing up, I never got the sense that he particularly liked me. I didn't feel *completely* unloved—if the house were on fire he would have dragged me out, though it would have been after he rescued everyone else. It could have been worse—at least I had my mother—but as a child it really bothered me. *What can I do to make him like me?* I used to wonder. The harder I tried to mold myself into the sort of son I thought he wanted, the more contemptuous he became, and so eventually I quit trying and founded the opposition party, which I still lead to this day. Whatever he's for, I'm against. Almost.

Watching my father asleep on my bed, I thought again of the pastel family portrait I'd ruined. If that were an isolated incident I might have a right to my self-pity, but if I'm honest about it, I wouldn't have liked my childhood self either. I regularly lied, and stole money from him. If there was silence in the car, I'd break it by making one of my sisters cry. "Dad, David keeps saying I'm pregnant and that the baby will have a cat's body and be born dead."

"I never—"

"Did too."

"Did not, liar."

For a while, when I was eleven or so, I used to drop the empty cardboard toilet rolls into the john. They would take a while to disappear, five or six flushes usually, but I was in no hurry.

The first three times the toilet clogged, my father went at it with the plunger, and that did the trick. Then, for some reason, the plunger wasn't enough. He ordered me to get his toolbox and to stand in the open doorway, ready to hand him whatever he called for. After draining the tank and turning off the water supply, he used his wrench on the lug nuts and unmoored the toilet from the floor, exposing a foul, corroded, fist-size hole that stunk up the entire house. I held my breath and watched as he reached down into it and withdrew part of the roll I had flushed a few hours earlier. "Who in the hell ... ?"

That night there was a big lecture at the dinner table. "When I get my hands on whoever's doing this ... "

He didn't even use a glove, I thought, watching as he took a piece of bread from the wicker basket we had.

A few nights later, I flushed another empty roll down the john, which clogged again. Out came the plunger, the tools, orders to stand in the doorway. The toilet was lifted off the floor, and as my father cursed and rolled up his sleeves, I must have laughed or at least smiled in some telltale way. "You," he growled, looking up at me from his kneeling position on the floor, "*you're* the one who's doing this?"

"Me?"

"Don't even try to talk your way out of it."

I offered some lame denial: "I hardly ever even *go* to the bathroom. You should ask Amy or Tiffany. They're the ones—"

"You are going to reach down into this pipe and pick out that cardboard roll," my father said. "Then you are never going to flush anything but toilet paper down this toilet again."

As I backed away, he pounced. Then he wrestled me to the floor, grabbed my hand, and forced it deep into what amounted to my family's asshole.

And there it has been ever since, sorting through our various shit. It's like I froze in that moment: with the same interests as that eleven-year-old boy, the same maturity level, the same haircut. The same glasses, even.

What I remember more vividly than the stench, and the sight of my hand when I pulled it out of that terrible pipe, was how strong my father was. I'd put up the fight of my life but might as well have been a doll, the way he wrenched apart my folded arms and took me by the wrist. I couldn't imagine being that powerful. He's slighter now, of course. Shorter by a few inches and downright skinny—arms and legs no thicker than the bones beneath them. *How was I ever afraid of this person?* I wondered now, watching his narrow chest as it rose and fell. "David!" he used to shout from the top of the stairs. "Get up here!"

"What did I do?" I'd call from my room, certain he'd found me out for something. "Whatever it was, it wasn't me."

141

"Get up here, now!"

Half the time it would be trouble—he'd discovered the branches ripped off the tree he'd just planted, or the football he gave me melted on the hibachi—but just as likely he'd be in the living room and music would be playing. It was always jazz, most often something on the radio. My father's most prized possession was his stereo system, which he housed in a glass-doored cabinet: turntable, amplifier, fancy tape deck, all of it top-of-the-line and off-limits to the rest of us.

"Sit down," he'd say, gesturing to the couch. "I want you to listen to this. I mean *really* listen."

I knew a guy in high school, Teetsil, who'd do the same thing. "There's this song you have to check out," he'd insist, taking *Born to Run* or some LP by the Who out of its jacket, filling his bedroom with the pleasant stink of new record.

Though I'd pretend otherwise—"Wow, great!"—nothing Teetsil played ever moved me or made me feel any better about the world I was living in. My dad, though, the things he exposed me to blew my mind. "Who is this?" I'd ask.

"Never mind that now, just listen."

He tried doing the same to my sisters and my brother, Paul, but none of them ever heard what he and I did. John Coltrane's "I Wish I Knew." Betty Carter singing "Beware My Heart." The hair on my arms would stand up, and everything else would recede—my shitty life at school, the loneliness and self-loathing I worried every day might drag me under—all of it replaced by unspeakable beauty. "Are you *getting* this?" he'd ask, his hands balled into fists the way a coach's might be, pacing the room as I listened. Afterward, spent, he'd turn down the volume, and we'd share that rare silence that was companionable rather than tense. *This* was what we had in common—music.

When he was growing up, jazz was the equivalent of rap or punk rock. Listening to it meant something. It made you a certain kind of person, especially to parents whose best-loved instrument was a bouzouki. I don't imagine Pappoú could have distinguished Miles Davis from a passing dump truck. It was all just noise to him. That might have been part of its appeal to my father, but it had nothing to do with mine. Music is the only way I *didn't* rebel against him.

Sitting in the silent afterglow of a song he'd just ordered me to listen to, I'd imagine myself onstage, sweat-drenched at the piano like Oscar Peterson, or perhaps I was the headlining trumpet player or guitarist taking a bow. The audience before me would be going wild with appreciation, though one person in particular would stand out—my father on his feet, cheering. "Did you *hear* that? That's my son up there!"

There was a baby grand piano just outside the bedroom I occupied until I left for college, and I'd strike the keys from time to time, imagining how proud I could make him by buckling down and really learning how to play. By the age of twelve, though, I knew a setup when I saw one. There's an expression you often hear from recovering alcoholics: Don't go to the hardware store for milk. If I were to master an instrument, or do anything creative with my life, I'd have to do it for myself, and myself only.

As an adult I regularly return to Raleigh and read out loud at what used to be Memorial Auditorium but is now part of the Duke Energy Center. My family will attend, and afterward—without fail—my father will say, "That was nice and everything, but it wasn't sold-out."

"Well, actually, it was," I'll tell him.

"No, it wasn't," he'll say. "While waiting for you to walk out onstage, I counted thirty empty seats."

This is him all over. The place accommodates more than 2,200 people, but all he can see are the unoccupied chairs.

"As a rule, five percent of concertgoers who buy their tickets six months or more in advance either forget to show up or make other plans in the meantime," I'll tell him, quoting my friend Adam, who started producing events thirty years ago and knows what he's talking about.

"That's not true," my father will say. "Those seats weren't forgotten. They were empty." This, as if a marked disinterest in me had turned them a different color.

"OK," I'll say, thinking, *Who does this—goes to the shows of people they're supposed to be proud of and counts the empty seats?*

Were I playing the piano to a packed house at the Monterey Jazz Festival, it would be no different. "Where the hell *was* everyone?" he'd ask when my set was over.

He takes a lot of naps now, my father. Two or three a day by my count, at least when we're all together at the beach. In twenty or so minutes he'd wake up, recharged, and though I wanted to join the action downstairs, I didn't want him to wake up in an empty room. There was nothing to do but wait, I supposed, and in the meantime I'd put together a playlist we could listen to. A little Jessica Williams, followed by Sam Jones and Eddie Higgins, people he might not have heard lately, a bill guaranteed to really shut us up for a while.

Untamed

Aside from Peter, who supposedly guards the gates of heaven and is a pivotal figure in any number of jokes, the only saint who's ever remotely interested me is Francis of Assisi, who was friends with the animals. I recall pictures of him, birds perched on his shoulders and his outstretched hands, deer at his feet, maybe a cougar in the background looking on and thinking, *There are some birds and deer I can kill, but wait . . . who's he?* Creatures gravitated to St. Francis because they recognized something in him, a quality that normal men lacked. *Let that be me,* I used to wish when I was ten and felt so desperately alone. There'd usually be a hamster clutched tight in my fist, trying with all his might to escape instead of resting companionably in my palm the way he was supposed to.

Skip ahead fifty years. It's late summer in West Sussex and I'm seated on the patio outside the converted stable I use as my office. It might be midnight or two a.m. I've brought out a lamp and set it on the table in front of me. To a casual observer, I'm tabulating receipts or writing letters, but what I'm really doing is waiting, almost breathlessly, for Carol.

I grew up in the suburbs of Raleigh, North Carolina, so didn't see a fox until I moved to France in 1998. There were plenty of them in Normandy, and every so often I'd come upon one, usually at dusk. It was hard to get a good look at them, since they'd run the moment they saw me, not as if they were frightened but as if they were guilty. This had to do with their heads, the way they were hanging, and their eyes, which were watchful but at the same time averted.

In Sussex too, foxes are common, though most of the ones I come upon are dead—hit by cars and rotting by the side of the road. The first time Hugh and I visited the area in 2010, we stayed with our friends Viv and Gretchen, who live in the village of Sutton. They'd roasted a chicken for dinner, and when we finished eating Viv threw the carcass into the yard. "For whoever wants it," he said.

When we got our own house, not far from theirs, we started doing the same thing: tossing our bones into the meadow our backyard opens onto. Whatever we put out vanishes by morning, but who or what took it is anyone's guess. We have badgers, but, as with foxes, you're more apt to come across them dead than alive. Occasionally I'll see a hedgehog on our property—Galveston, his name is—and there's no shortage of deer and partridge. We have pheasant and stoats and so many rabbits that in the spring and summer it looks as if our house is the backdrop for an Easter commercial.

One of the reasons I don't want a cat is that it will kill our wildlife. My brother has to change his doormat every two months—that's how much his savages drag home—and my sister Gretchen's are just as bad. She's forever returning from work to find a chipmunk on her sofa, its head chewed to a paste, or a bird that's not quite dead flapping the stump that used to be a wing against her blood-spattered kitchen floor.

Another argument against pets—at least for Hugh and me—are the fights they lead to. In the mid-nineties we got two cats, the last of thirty owned by the actress Sandy Dennis, who had recently died of ovarian cancer and who had lived in a house in Connecticut that, on a summer day, you could smell from our apartment in SoHo. Angel and Barratos were black with white spots, both short-haired. We changed their names to Sandy and Dennis, and from the day they entered our lives until the day they died, Hugh and I fought over how to feed and care for them.

I'm of the "Let's-fatten-you-up-until-you're-too-obese-to-do-much-of-anything" school, while he's more practical, or "mean," as I'm apt to call it. "You don't know what it's like, living in a small apartment day and night with nothing to look forward to," I used to say. "All they live for is food, so why not give it to them?"

This "healthy pet" nonsense—I just don't buy it. I can't tell you how many times I've gone to a neighbor with a bag of left-overs, only to be told that their dog doesn't "do" table scraps. And bones—no way. "He could choke!"

These are the same people who avoid canned food in favor of dry nuggets that remain in the bowl, ignored, for days at a time but are, I'm told, "so-o-o-o-o much better for him than that other stuff."

I once knew someone in New York who insisted that his black Lab was a vegetarian.

"Just like you," I said. "Gosh, what a coincidence!"

When the dog charged after a hamburger someone had dropped on the sidewalk outside a McDonald's on Eighth Avenue, he was, I guess, just going after the pickle.

Then there are all the behavioral arguments that joint pet ownership leads to: "Don't let her jump up on the table/countertop/stereo," etc. As if you can stop a cat from going where she likes. That's why you want them fifteen pounds overweight. It keeps them lower to the ground.

Sandy was old and died a year after we got her. We brought Dennis to France when we left New York and shuttled him between the house in Normandy and the apartment in Paris. This led to regular fights over how to get him into his cat carrier, and how often to let him outside. When he died, we fought over where to bury him, and how deep.

All I can say is: Thank God we never had children. We

even fight about the creatures I drag home—things I find, most often, on my walks and wrap up in a handkerchief. They're usually mice or shrews, already doomed, though not by anything obvious: They haven't been run over. There are never any teeth marks on them. Perhaps they're diseased or just too old to run away from me.

"You're not giving it *croutons,* are you?" Hugh will say. "'It' is named Canfield, and I'm not forcing him to eat any-thing," I'll answer, dropping what will look like a fistful of dice into the terrarium or, if that's already in use as a hospice for some dying toad or vole, my backup bucket. "They're just there if he wants them."

Onto this battleground, Carol arrived. "It's the funniest thing," Hugh said one evening in mid-July. "I had the kitchen door open earlier and this little fox walked by, looked in at me, and continued on her way. Not run-ning, not in any hurry. She looks to me like she might be named Carol."

The next afternoon I threw a steak bone into the pasture, and at dusk I glanced out and saw a fox with it in her mouth. "Hugh," I called, "come look."

At the sound of my voice, the fox—most certainly the Carol I'd been hearing about—returned the bone to the ground, the way you might if you were caught trying to shoplift something. "I was just ... seeing how ... heavy this was," she seemed to say, before taking off.

The following night we ate chicken at the table on the

patio outside my office. It was dusk, and just as we finished there was Carol. One of the things I've come to appreciate is that you never see her coming. Rather, she simply appears. When she reached a distance of six feet or so, I threw her the bones off my plate. "What are you *doing?*" Hugh hissed as she commenced eating them.

Here we go, I thought.

Once a week during this past summer I'd stay awake all night, tying up loose ends. I liked the way I was left feeling at dawn—not tired but just the opposite: speedy, almost, and brilliant. Not long after the chicken dinner, I was working at my outdoor table when, at around four a.m., Carol showed up. We had no meat in the refrigerator, but she waited while I found some cheese and opened a tin of sardines.

Foxes often bury their food, saving it for later. I thought that meant a day or two, but apparently there's nothing they consider too spoiled. Rotten is acceptable, as is putrid. Since we met Carol, our backyard has become a graveyard for pork chops and beef jerky and raw chicken legs. "What's *this?*" Hugh demanded not long ago. He was on his knees in a flower bed, a trowel in one hand and what looked like a desiccated thumb in the other.

I squinted in his direction. "Um, half a hot dog?"

He was furious. "What are you *doing?* Foxes don't want junk like this. Hot dogs are disgusting."

"Not to someone who eats *maggots,*" I said.

He claims that I'm manipulating Carol. "That's you, the

puppet master. It's the same way you are with people—constantly trying to buy them."

He's under the impression that the occasional chicken carcass is enough, that anything else will "spoil" Carol—will, in fact, endanger her. "Believe me, she was just fine before you came along."

But was she? Really? It's a hard life out there for a fox. Yes, there are rabbits and birds around, but they don't surrender easily. According to the websites I've visited, Carol's diet consists mainly of beetles and worms. There's an occasional mouse, and insect larvae, maybe some roadkill—just awful-tasting stuff.

"And I'm willing to bet that all those same websites advise against feeding wild animals," Hugh said.

"Well, not *all* of them," I told him.

They do discourage hand-feeding, not because you'll be bitten but because, once tame, the fox is likely to approach your neighbor, who may not be as receptive to his or her company as you are. I can see how that might be a problem in America, where everyone has a gun, but in England, what are you going to do, stab Carol to death? Good luck getting that close, because the only person she really trusts is *me*.

You should see the way she follows me to the garden bench, almost as if she were a dog but at the same time catlike, nimble, her tail straight out and bobbing slightly as she walks. Then she'll lie on the grass at my feet, her paws crossed, and look at me for a second before turning away. Carol's uncomfortable making eye contact—a shame, as hers have the brilliance of freshly minted pennies. From nose to tail her coloring is remarkable: the burnt orange fading to what looks like a white bib protecting her chest, then darkening from rust to black on her front legs, which resemble spent matchsticks. Because I give her only the best ground beef and free-range chicken, her coat is full, not mangy like those other foxes'. Carol has come as close as two inches from my hand, butI have to look away as she approaches. Again, it's the eye-contact thing.

In pictures she looks like a stuffed animal. And, oh, I show them to everyone. "Have you seen my fox? No? Hold on while I get my phone ... " In my favorite photograph she's outside the kitchen door. It's around seven in the evening, still light, and you can see her perfectly, just sitting there. It's actually Hugh who took the picture, so the expression on her face says, "Yes, but where's *David?*"

The response to my photos is wonderment tinged with envy: "How come *I* don't have a Carol?" Unless, of course, the person I'm speaking to is small-minded. A lot of small-minded people out where we live raise chickens.

"Horrible, brutal things, foxes," they say. "Once one gets into the henhouse it'll kill everything in sight, just for the hell of it."

The charge was repeated in the comments section of a YouTube video I watched one night about a vixen named Tammy that was hit by a car and healed by a veterinarian, who later released her back into the wild. "I know how much people love to save wildlife, but how would you feel if a fox killed your chickens or turkey?" someone named Pat Stokes asked.

To this a man responded, "My chickens are cunts."

I don't know if this made him pro-fox or if he was just stating the facts.

If I had to bad-mouth Carol, my one complaint would be her sense of humor. "You are so-o-o-o-o serious," I often tell her. I'd add that she never grows any more comfortable in my presence. She seems to me very English in her awkwardness.

"Then stop making her uncomfortable," Hugh says. He thinks that, instead of feeding her on the patio outside my office, I should leave her food in the field and let her eat it on her own time.

The first problem with that suggestion is slugs. I thought I knew them from my youth in Raleigh, but the slugs of North America are nothing compared to their British cousins. They're like walruses in Sussex—long and fat from eating everything Hugh tries to grow that the rabbits and deer happen to miss. I've seen them feast on the viscous bodies of their stepped-on relatives, so when something decent is presented, pork shoulder, say, or a fresh lamb kidney, they go wild. And we must have—no exaggeration—at least twelve million slugs on our two-acre property. Galveston the hedgehog keeps their numbers down, as do two toads, Lane and Courtney, but it's a losing battle.

The second problem with throwing food into the pasture is one of perception. It would allow Carol to feel, if not like a huntress, then at least like a successful scavenger—*Look what I found,* she'd think. This as opposed to, *Look what David gave me.*

I insist that Carol eat in my presence for the same reason I wait for the coffee shop employee to turn back in my direction before putting a tip in his basket. I want to be acknowledged as a generous provider. This is about *me,* not them.

I don't need Hugh to point out how ridiculous this is. Wild animals do not give a damn about our little feelings. They're incapable of it. "I love you, I love you, I love you," we say.

What they hear is senseless noise. It's like us trying to discern emotion in the hum of a hair dryer or the chortle of an engine as it fails to turn over. That's the drawback but also the glory of creatures that were never domesticated. Nothing feels better than being singled out by something that at best should fear you and at worst would like to eat you. I think of the people I've known over the years who've found a baby raccoon or possum and brought it home to raise it. When young, the animals were sweet. Then one day they became moody and violent, like human teenagers but with claws and sharp, pointy teeth. It was their wildness reclaiming them. After the change it was back into their cages, their heartsick owners—jailers now—watching as they tore at the bars, never tiring of it, thinking only of escape.

But wait, we tell ourselves, always wanting to project, to anthropomorphize, to turn the story in our favor. *But what about this:* One night in late September, as I was walking home in the dark from the neighboring village, I felt a presence next to me. *A dog?* I wondered. But the footsteps I heard were daintier, and I wasn't near any houses. I keep a flashlight in my backpack, so I turned it on, and there was Carol. "Is this where you are when I call for you at two in the morning?" I asked.

There was a canopy of leaves over my head. Once I moved beyond it, the moon lit my path, so I turned off the flashlight. I'd expected Carol to be gone by that point, but for the next half mile, all the way home, she walked with me, sometimes by my side and sometimes a few steps ahead, leading the way. No cars approached or passed. The road was ours, and we marched right down the center of it, all the way to the front of the house and through the garden gate to the kitchen door.

I didn't know it then, but this would be the last time I would see Carol. Foxes are like gang members. They can't go wherever they like. That next patch of land is someone else's territory, so chances are she was killed somehow. If she'd been hit by a car I'd have seen her body by the side of the road, but maybe she dragged herself off into the woods and died there. She could have been poisoned, which happens. Hunters pay good money to bag the pheasant that are released here every fall. These are birds that, honestly, you have to work *not to* kill. The landowners want to protect their investments, which means keeping down the predators. "That's likely what happened to Carol," Hugh says. I know this makes sense, but I refuse to hear it.

She's just taking a little break, I think. *Trying to establish her independence, which is normal for someone her age.* I still call for her when I step into the yard at night. Still look into the shadows for some hint of movement, waiting to change my tone from the voice you use when summoning someone, to the less plaintive and much more preferable one you use to welcome them back home.

The One(s) Who Got Away

It was a Friday night in mid-July, around nine o'clock, and Hugh and I were at the dinner table, eating this spaghetti he makes with sausage in it. We'd been together for almost three decades, and for some reason I'd waited until this moment to ask how many people he'd slept with before we became a couple.

Hugh looked at the ceiling, which is crisscrossed with beams and, to my great consternation, spiderwebs. I'm vigilant, really I am, but out in the country there's no keeping up with them.

"So?" I said.

"I'm thinking," he told me.

I used to know how many people I'd slept with. After

159

meeting Hugh, though, I took myself off the market, and the figure faded from memory. If I were to slog through all my old diaries I could certainly retrieve it. Twenty-eight? Thirty? Do I include those early gropings? They felt significant at the time, but do they qualify as sex if you never took your clothes off or actually touched anything with your bare hands? I wanted to ask Hugh, but he was too busy counting. "Thirty-two, thirty-three . . . "

I put down my fork. "You're not finished yet?"

"Shhh," he said. "You're making me lose track."

It shouldn't have surprised me. When you look like Hugh, all you have to do is leave the house and people will approach you, especially gay men, the dogs. His handsomeness was never my personal opinion—rather, like the roundness of the earth, it is something society generally agrees upon. Without my face to use as bait, I had to work a lot harder than he did. There are times, I'll admit, when I had to beg. That said, some of Hugh's earlier choices seemed poorly thought-out to me, especially once AIDS came along.

"Thirty-five . . . thirty-six."

Every man ticked off on his fingers was someone I'd been compared to at one point or another, not overtly—he's anything but cruel—but surely it happened. Someone kissed better than I did. Someone had more stamina, a more seductive voice. Bigger muscles. I'm confident enough to compete against a dozen of his exes, but he was moving on to the population of a small town.

"Thirty-eight, thirty-nine . . . " By what miracle had

neither of us contracted AIDS? How had we gotten away? I don't just mean later, when people knew to be safe, but back in the days when it didn't have a name and no one understood how it spread. One of the men Hugh had lived with—a professor he had his first year of college—had died of it in the late eighties, and surely there were others, on both my side and his. Yet for some reason we'd escaped, had prospered, even. Now here we were, the shadows lengthening, our spaghetti growing cold, as he hit the half-hundred mark, then blithely sailed beyond it.

Whore.

Sorry

When she was young, my sister-in-law, Kathy, had a kitten named Snowy. "She was white, of course," she said one evening over the Sorry! board at our house on Emerald Isle. I've never been much for games, but this one I can play all night. Half of it is luck, and the rest is ruthlessness. You have to be cold, so my niece, Madelyn, who is twelve and has a heart made of frozen concrete, usually wins.

"She was just the prettiest thing," Kathy continued, watching as I shuffled the deck for another round. "Then she swallowed a fishhook."

I set the cards in the center of the board. "Yikes."

"Tell me about it," Kathy said. "It didn't seem like there was any way to fix her, so my mom told my brother to hold her down." She took a sip of her bourbon. "Then she shot her in the head."

Maddy, who had no doubt heard this story before, gathered the bright plastic pawns in her hands and turned to her mother, asking, "What color do you want?"

Kathy considered her options and sighed. "I'll go with the red."

Whenever I doubt the wisdom of buying a beach house, all I have to do is play a round of Sorry! and it all seems worth it. For starters, it's the only time Madelyn will really talk. Wiping the floor with everyone around her eases what is otherwise a crippling shyness and brings her fully to life. Ask her a question on the beach, and the most you're likely to get is a shrug. At the board, on the other hand, she'll tell you anything, is chatty, almost. Before getting the Sea Section, I didn't have much contact with my brother's family. I'd see them in Raleigh when I passed through town every other year. I'd send cards and letters, but that was about it. Were it not for Sorry! I'd never have known that Kathy's mother shot a kitten in the head. *Now that's a sister-in-law,* I thought. She drew a one, and I watched as she moved the first of her four pawns from the starting position. Then she whispered softly to me and her daughter, "I will destroy the both of you."

We usually play Sorry! in the living room on the east side of the house while sitting on the floor around the coffee table. Getting a game together is the easiest thing in the world. Only four at a time can play, but there will often be others on the sidelines, coaching—Paul, for instance. When his daughter's at the board he'll take a knee and lean in. "C'mon, baby, go for the throat. Just like Daddy taught you."

It's hard to get ahead in this game without occasionally sending a fellow player back to start. "Sorry," you say, sincerely at first, and then in a way that means "I'm sorry you're the sort of person who deserves this." Madelyn will take any opportunity to screw someone over. She's like her grandmother shooting a kitten in the head—heartless. The Christmas that Paul brought his family to Sussex, she presented me with a Sorry! game of my own, and though we pulled it out a dozen or so times, it never felt urgent, the way it does at the beach. After they left, I played only once, with a friend of Hugh's named Candy. "You sort of need the sound of waves in order to get in the proper mood," I said, putting the board away after I had crushed her.

Another thing I love about the beach is sitting in the sun, mainly for the lazy kind of talk it generates. A person can say anything with lotion on, and I'm more than willing to listen. Most people, myself included, have moved on to sunblock, but not my sister Gretchen, who is outdoors a lot and usually arrives at the start of our vacation the burnished chestnut of a well-worn saddle. This is a woman who tans the spaces between her fingers, who lies on the beach with her mouth open so she can darken the front of her uvula. She's starting to look like one of those dolls made from a dried apple, not that it bothers her any. My sister is one of the few women I

165

know who doesn't dye her hair or bemoan the fact that she's getting older. She embraces her impending decrepitude.

Gretchen's birthday falls in early August, and the year she turned fifty-five, we celebrated it together on Emerald Isle. Paul, Kathy, and Madelyn were there briefly, as was Hugh; his mother, Joan; and his sister, Ann, who is my age and has three grown children. She and Hugh could be twins, that's how alike they look, both tall and slender with big teeth, just shy of Kennedy-size. Their mother is a lot smaller, and wispy. Joan is eighty-three now, pale as a lightbulb, with white hair cut bluntly at her jawline. She recently replaced her wire-rimmed glasses. The new ones have heavy black frames and lend her a studious, almost owlish demeanor, which is fitting, as she's always got her nose in a book. The writers she prefers are long dead and were on the wordy side. If the novel on the sofa is seven hundred pages long and the author photo is an engraving, it's either hers or Hugh's.

One of the differences between his family and my own is the way we'll listen to a story. It's hard to finish more than a few sentences at a time when talking to his mother, who likes to interrupt either to accuse you of exaggerating—"Oh, now, *that's* not true"—or to defend the person you're talking about, someone, most often, she has never met. A stranger could hit me across the face with a sawed-off table leg, then kick me until my spinal column snapped, and still Joan would say, "Well, I'm sure he meant well."

My family, on the other hand, is always happy to hear about how horrible someone is. You could wake any of my sisters from a sound sleep, say, "You won't believe what this asshole said to me once in 1979," and have her full attention. Not Joan, though. Or her daughter either. Tell Ann that you want the renters two doors down—the ones who blast country music from their boom box and howl, "Yeee-ha!" every two minutes—to die, and she'll say, "You should never wish ill on people. That's bad karma!"

Around the Hamricks, you can't even denigrate sharks, which were on everyone's mind in the summer of 2015. By the time we arrived, they had attacked eight swimmers, most of them in shallow water. People were canceling their vacation rentals, and it got even worse after two kids, one aged twelve and the other sixteen, had their arms bitten off.

"Yes, well, the sharks didn't *eat* those arms," Hugh said when I brought it up. To him this somehow made it better, though I didn't see it that way at all. In fact, it made it worse. Why dismember young people for no reason?

"Besides," Hugh said, "I go out far when I swim."

"Right, but in order to *get* to where it's deep you sort of have to pass through the shallow part."

"But I can do that quickly," he argued. "Anyway, sharks don't want *me*. They want fish."

It was clear I was wasting my breath. I said to Gretchen, "I just pray they get his left arm instead of his right one. That way he can still kind of cook."

*

You can issue all the warnings you like, but nothing will keep a Hamrick out of the ocean. She's frail, Hugh's mother, a bit wobbly now, yet twice a day her children would lead her beyond the waves, one at each elbow, steadying her until they reached the calm water. Then they'd let go, and the three of them would swim for an hour at a time.

Gretchen and I watched them from the shore one afternoon, me gessoed with sunblock, and her glistening with what may have been bacon fat. The sight of Joan backstroking off into the distance made us think of our own mother. She would wade knee-deep in the ocean if she were fishing, but we never saw her go any farther. Even at the country club the most she'd do is stick her feet in the kiddie pool. She didn't know how to swim. No one ever taught her. "Plus," said Gretchen, "she didn't want to get her hair wet."

Time spent underwater would have been less time our mother had to observe people and discuss their shortcomings in a group setting. She even did it to us, her own children. "You won't believe what Lisa's done this time," she'd whisper to me in the kitchen or living room, her cigarette stalled an inch from her mouth while this much more important business took place. Being her confidant made me feel special: only she and I could truly understand how stupid the people in my family were. The downside, I discovered, was that no one was safe. It was hurtful the first few times her criticism got back to me. ("I don't know who he thinks he's fooling with that Raquel Welch poster.") Then I realized that it didn't mean anything. Opinions constantly shifted and evolved, were fluid the same way thoughts were. Ten minutes into *The Exorcist* you might say, "This is boring." An hour later you could decide that it was the best thing you'd ever seen, and it was no different with people. The villain at three in the afternoon might be the hero by sunset. It was all just storytelling.

Try explaining that to a Hamrick, though. "After I die, and you read something bad about yourself in my diary, do yourself a favor and keep reading," I often say to Hugh. "I promise that on the next page you'll find something flattering. Or maybe the page after that."

Now I stood and waved to him out in the water. As I sat back down, Gretchen reached for her iPod and told me about a group of teenagers she recently ran into at the grocery store near her house. "They were fourteen, maybe fifteen years old, laughing and pushing each other—just awful, right? So I went over and told them to shut up."

I took off my shirt and balled it up for use as a pillow. "Wow."

"I know it," Gretchen said. "Normally I wouldn't have gotten involved. Then, of course, they wound up behind me in line, still loud and obnoxious, and almost like there was someone else inhabiting my body, I turned around and said, 'Did I not tell you to *shut the fuck up?*'"

"Then what happened?" I asked.

She lit a cigarette and shrugged. "They shut the fuck up."

*

That night at the Sorry! board, Kathy told me that she and Madelyn had stopped by the pier earlier in the day and watched as people fed the sharks. "There must have been ten of them, some as long as five feet," she said.

"Are you hearing this?" I called to Hugh. He was sitting on the porch with his mother and sister, no doubt recalling the time they chased a hippo from their tennis court back when they lived in the Congo. God, those Hamricks can reminisce. "Kathy saw twenty-five sharks, some of them twelve feet long, at the pier this afternoon."

"Now, that's not true," Joan said.

"Even if she did see them, the pier is at least a mile from here," Hugh added.

"Sharks do this thing called 'swimming,'" I told him. "A mile is nothing to them."

I turned to Madelyn, who had drawn a ten and, instead of moving forward like a normal, sweet sixth-grader, employed the card's other option and took one step back, thereby returning my pawn to start, though I posed no threat to her whatsoever.

"You will grow up to be a terrible person," I told her. "I mean, more terrible than you are now. If that's even possible."

"He didn't mean that," Joan called from out on the porch.

My goal on this beach trip was to find the snapping turtle I'd befriended the previous summer and feed him the lipoma I'd had cut out of me in El Paso. It had been in the freezer for nine months now, in a ziplock bag with DAVID'S TUMOR written on it. Every day I'd go down to the canal and stand on the narrow footbridge. The snapper I was searching for was as big as my rolling suitcase and had a hideous growth, a little top hat of flesh cocked just so on his head. There was no mistaking him for anyone else—that's what I liked about him. He had style.

I mentioned him at the Sorry! board, and Madelyn, not caring that I'd called her a terrible person, said, "Didn't Daddy tell you? That turtle is dead." It seems she and Paul had gone looking for him earlier in the summer and were given the news by the man who lives beside the bridge and who had apparently found the body. So there went that.

Still, there was no reason to let a perfectly good lipoma go to waste. And so I went in search of another candidate. The one I chose lurks behind a shopping plaza. A lot of turtles congregate there—not just snappers but sliders as well—because vacationers feed them. There's a coin-operated machine that dispenses what looks like dried dog food, so kids will buy a fistful and drop the pellets piece by piece into the water ten feet below. Others skip the dispenser and toss in their leftovers from the two nearby restaurants. French fries, onion rings, pizza crusts—the turtles will eat anything.

The day I brought out my defrosted tumor, a dozen or so people were gathered around the railing. I reached into my ziplock bag, realizing as I did so that what I was touching was myself, or what used to be myself. The egg-size lipoma had been diced into ten or so pieces and was greasy and blood-soaked, not like anything I'd put my hands on before. I threw a dollop to the fiercest of the five snapping turtles idling among the pylons, and he ate it with gusto. Then I threw in another bit, and another after that. Beside me stood a potbellied man in a baseball cap. His shirt had short sleeves and was unbuttoned almost to the waist. "I don't know what you're feeding that guy, but he's sure loving it."

I nodded.

He looked at my ziplock bag. "What *is* that, by the way?"

I emptied the last few bits and, realizing how complicated it would be to answer "My tumor," I said instead, "Nothing much. Just some raw chicken."

I'd brought a damp paper towel to wash my hands with, but my lipoma was messier than I'd anticipated, so I went to the Food Lion that's attached to the shopping center to buy some wet wipes. The store was crowded with vacationers, renters who, grocery-wise, were having to start from scratch: salt and pepper, cooking oil, aluminum foil, ketchup. Carts were heaped. I got into the express line behind a middle-aged man in a T-shirt. I never saw the front of it, but the back pictured a Labrador retriever standing on the beach with a bikini top in his mouth. Below him were the words good dog.

Some people, I thought, opening the wet wipes so I could wash the tumor off my hands before I touched my wallet.

Over a game of Sorry! that night, I told Kathy and Madelyn about the turtle I'd thrown my lipoma to. I had four pawns on the board, more than anyone else, but it was too early to start gloating. Fortunes can reverse in a matter of seconds, especially when my niece is around. "I thought I'd be able to feed him a kidney as well, but it fell through," I said, praying as my sister-in-law reached for a card that it wouldn't have the word SORRY! written on it.

Kathy drew a useless twelve. "A kidney from a dog or cat?"

"No," I said. "From a human teenager."

Madelyn drew a one and released the first of her four pawns from the starting gate. "Who was the teenager?"

"A sixteen-year-old I met in Albuquerque last spring," I said. "The two of us got to talking, and when I asked if he was getting a summer job, he said no, that after school got out he'd be checking into the hospital. One of his kidneys was dead inside him, so he was going to have it removed."

Kathy looked up and frowned. "Poor guy."

"There was something special about him," I told her. "He was funny and remarkably articulate for someone his age. I asked if he had an iPad, and when he told me no, I said, 'Well, you do now. I'm buying you one so you can use it in the hospital.'"

"Wow," Kathy said. "That was really nice of you."

"Wasn't it?" I took a moment to feel good about myself. "In exchange he promised me his dead kidney, though I knew it was a long shot. Goddamn doctors. I understand not giving him the entire thing—it would be a lot to carry—but the least they could have done was break off a corner."

"I don't think kidneys have corners," Madelyn said.

"Don't be such a know-it-all," I told her. "It's a really bad trait for a child."

I'd think back on this exchange the following day, after I'd repeated the story about the iPad to Hugh's mother. You're not supposed to talk about your good deeds, I know. It effectively negates them and in the process makes people hate you. If there's a disaster, for instance, and someone tells me he donated five thousand dollars to the relief effort—this while I gave a lesser amount, or nothing at all—I don't think, *Goodness, how bighearted you are,* but, rather, *Fuck you for making me look selfish.*

That said, Hugh's mother could have given me a little more credit. What I got instead was "You bought a brand-new iPad for some kid you don't even know? Now, that's just showing off."

"Now hold on a minute—," I said.

"If you really want to help someone, you should think about those Syrian refugees," she continued.

"I know, but—"

"I see them on TV, some of them drowning, their children dead, and it just tears me apart. That's who you should be reaching out to, not some American who probably has a car and who knows what else."

Syria, like Kosovo before it, was one of those stories that started while I wasn't paying attention or, rather, while I was paying attention to something else—a celebrity wedding, perhaps. Then all of a sudden it was everywhere and I felt it was too late to get into it. The teenager, on the other hand, was right in front of me. Doing something nice for him was easy and immediate and didn't lead to the mountain of junk mail you're punished with whenever you give to an established charity.

We had lunch on the deck that afternoon—a salad with shrimp in it. As Hugh brought it to the table, his sister recounted the flight she and Joan had taken from Louisville. There was nothing much to her story—she'd asked a woman to swap seats so she could sit beside her mother, and the woman, quite logically to my mind, said no.

All I do is fly, so one-upping Ann was pretty easy. "A few years back, at a book signing, I met a pilot," I began. "He flew the Newark to Palm Beach route, right? So it's December twenty-third, and as they touch down in Florida, one of the flight attendants takes the microphone and delivers her standard landing speech. 'Please remain seated until the FASTEN SEAT BELT sign has been turned off and be careful when opening the overhead bins. We'd like to wish you a merry Christmas and, to those of you already standing, happy Hanukkah.'"

Joan put down her fork. "Oh, now, she didn't say that!"

"Why not?" I asked.

"Because it's prejudiced."

"Of course it is, but that doesn't mean she didn't say it."

"Well, that's just nonsense," Joan continued. "That never happened. The pilot was just pulling your leg."

I hate being challenged over a story someone told me. "Really?" I asked. "And do you know him? Were you there?"

"No, but—"

"So actually," I said, my heart racing as I pushed myself away from the table, "you have no idea what you're talking about, do you?"

Hugh's opening line when scolding me afterward in the privacy of our bedroom was "How dare you talk to my mother that way."

I tried to explain why it had so bothered me, and he cut me off. "What's it like to know that the best part of yourself just got fed to a snapping turtle?"

I then reminded him of the time my father came for Christmas. "It was 1998 in Normandy, and you told him to get the fuck out of your kitchen."

Hugh crossed his arms. "Again, you're wrong. What I said was 'I *need for you* to get the fuck out of my kitchen.'"

"That's not better," I said. "It's just . . . longer."

He insisted I apologize to his mother, and then he stomped into the storage room in search of something—his cloak of self-righteousness, maybe. After he'd left, I changed into my bathing suit and joined my sister on her beach blanket. It was early afternoon, hot and bright. Gretchen was wearing a fudge-colored tankini that disappeared against her skin and made it look like she was naked. "Is that the swimsuit you bought the time we went to Hawaii together?" I asked, still stinging from my most recent arguments. Joan was right, of course, I had been showing off, but so what?

A truly decent kid got an iPad out of it. It made him happy, and if it made *me* happy to tell a few dozen people about it, or, OK, a few thousand, what was the harm? As for the story the pilot told me, why would he have made it up? Why does everything that counters Joan's worldview have to be false? Bad things happen: People are discriminated against and tortured. Kittens swallow fishhooks and get shot in the head. I'm not saying you should dwell solely on the negative, but why blot it out entirely, especially in a social setting where it's practically your duty to spark debate and lively conversation?

Then too, why am *I* always the one to apologize? It wouldn't kill me to return to the house and say I'm sorry, but I couldn't have said it with any conviction. It would, in fact, make me the liar I'd just been accused of being, and how was that fair?

The people two doors down who'd been playing country music since we arrived had left, finally. Just as I was appreciating how quiet it was, a rescue helicopter appeared from the sound side of the island and soared off over the water, perhaps looking for a drowning victim or some poor swimmer who'd been mauled by a shark. It's beautiful, the Atlantic, but at the same time so insistent, always advancing, always taking what it wants. When the helicopter eventually disappeared over the horizon, I meant to recount my recent battles with Hugh and his mother, to tap into the comfort and outrage that only my family can provide, but just as I opened my mouth, Gretchen sat up and said, lazily, almost like someone who was talking in her sleep, "Do you remember my old boyfriend Greg?"

"Sure."

She lit a cigarette and took a deep draw. "He used to drink the liquid out of tuna cans." The story of my argument was insignificant now, dwarfed by this larger and infinitely more fascinating topic. I let go of my anger, all of it, and leaned back on the beach blanket, feeling palpably lighter, giddy almost. Feeling related. "Oil or water?" I asked.

Gretchen leaned back as well and brought her cigarette to her sun-blistered lips. "Both."

Boo-Hooey

If there's one thing I can't stand, it's people talking about ghosts. You wouldn't think it would be that much of a problem—"Who are you hanging out with, for God's sake?" someone might ask. "Camp counselors?"—but even friends I'd thought of as normal have something to say when the talk, as it invariably does, turns to haunted houses. Or apartments. Or dorm rooms. Or secondhand suitcases.

Leading the charge is usually Hugh. Don't get him started on the farmhouse he and his family lived in after returning to the United States in the late 1970s, or you'll never hear the end of it. And if his mother's in the room at the same time, run. Though they sometimes argue over whether this particular ghost was wearing a red dress or a blue one with tiny checks, they're generally in accord over her haunting style. She wasn't a chain rattler. She wasn't "aggressive," but neither did she keep out of sight. "The poor thing," Hugh's mother says. "Trapped between one world and the next—it can't be easy."

"There must be spirits in your house," people say when they visit Hugh and me in England. "A place this old has got to be crawling with them."

"Nope," I say. "Sorry."

I thought the ghosts these people were referring to would have died in one of the bedrooms—a consumptive child, maybe, or a grandmother with buckshot wounds. But according to my sister Amy, who heard it from a reliable source, spirits can just as easily be brought in. "They travel in antiques sometimes," she said.

"Like dressers and corner cupboards?" I asked.

"Or picture frames or candlesticks," she explained. "They can attach themselves to just about anything. That's why a lot of people won't wear vintage clothes."

I thought she was making this up, but it's a real thing, apparently. "Dry-cleaning doesn't kill them?" I asked.

"They're not bedbugs," Amy said. "They're ghosts!"

Hugh claims the reason I've never seen one is that I'm not perceptive enough. This is his way of telling me that I'm self-centered, suggesting that if I weren't so concerned about, for example, meeting my daily Fitbit goal, I'd realize there's a six-hundred-year-old milkmaid living in our silverware drawer. He's saying that he, his mother, and all the other people who detect flickering shadows on their bedroom walls are special in a way that I am not.

"And what about people who see pixies?" I ask.

"Well, they're just crazy," Hugh says.

If there are no ghosts in your home or office, if your parking deck and toolshed are spirit-free, you don't have to feel left out. There are any number of places that advertise themselves as haunted—inns and such. "Did you see Headless Hazel?" the owners ask over breakfast, no doubt silently chuckling as guests cry, "I did! She was at the end of the hall when we came up from dinner last night, stabbing a doll with a knitting needle!"

I refuse to support the poltergeist industry, so would sooner sleep in a cardboard box than at the Belle Grove Plantation or the Albert Shafsky House, or any of the other places listed in the Hundred Most Haunted Hotels and B&Bs in America, none of which is named the Scarriott for some reason.

The number two thing I can't stand hearing about are dreams. "How did you sleep?" I'll sometimes ask Hugh.

If his answer has anything to do with piloting a plane made of meat, or handing a poker chip the size of a trash-can lid to a sea lion with Yoko Ono's face, I'll either put my fingers in my ears or walk out of the room.

David Sedaris

All that said, I do believe the dead can visit us in our sleep—though not in anything I'd call a dream, and not in a form I'd consider in any way "ghostly." Take my mother, for instance. Every time I see her she's seated at a table in an otherwise empty room. She is never outlandishly dressed. She's not transparent or oversize or tiny. The tone of our visits is almost formal. She asks how things are going, and I answer the same way I would if I were awake. Like, for example, when I quit smoking. She wondered what was new, and I held up my empty hand.

"Wow," she said, noticing the cigarette that wasn't there. "How'd you do that?"

The longest she ever quit was for two weeks. "I just wasn't strong enough to put it behind me," she said.

"Well," I told her, "don't beat yourself up over it. I suppose it was all part of what made you *you*."

In our visits my mother is always sixty-two, the age she was when she died. In 1991 that seemed old to me, though now, of course, I'm almost there myself. Before I know it, she and I will be contemporaries. Then I'll overtake her, and how strange will that be, to have a mother young enough to be my daughter? When that day comes, will I think her naive? "What do you know about being old?" I'll ask, me with white hair or, likelier still, bald. "You never even reached retirement age!"

Already there's so much she's missed out on: email; ISIS; reality TV; my niece, Madelyn. I have to watch what I say—otherwise I spend half my visit explaining what something is.

"They're pictures you take of yourself with a phone and send to the people you no longer communicate with by talking."

When it's time for my mother to go, she stands up and brushes her hands on her skirt. Sometimes she has her big beige purse with her and sometimes not. Her hair is always done. She's made-up and has her octagonal glasses on. We hug, and then she leaves, not eagerly but not regretfully either. It's the same with Tiffany, though she tends to stand rather than sit. My sister was never what you'd call a big listener, but in my sleep she's all ears. "Really?" she'll say. "And then what?"

In fact, we never talk about her. Just me.

"That's how you know it's a dream," Amy says.

But it's not, it's *real*. I'm not alone in this. It happens to other people as well, and unlike with a nightmare or a ghost story, I don't mind hearing about it. "I talked to my dad last night," Hugh will tell me at least once a year.

"Give me the details," I'll say, as I liked his father. Sam could be intimidating, but he was an original thinker when it came to politics. "Did he talk about the election?" I'll ask. "Oh, he must be furious."

I can never predict when Tiffany or my mother will show up. I can't conjure them, nor can I control how long they stay. The following morning I'll feel content, recharged. When I think of Mom or my sister the day after a visit, I remember only the good times and wish it could always be this way. I don't like recalling their faults or the arguments we had, though with my mother there were only a handful, and they were usually over within an hour or so.

I wonder if, after I'm dead, I'll be able to visit people the way my mother and sister can. It's nice to think I could drop in on Hugh and tell him to keep his chin up. I've told him a thousand times that after I'm gone he needs to find himself a new boyfriend. I've even identified some. The first two, OK, maybe I didn't put enough thought into them. "Are you *kidding?*" Hugh said when I pointed out Gilles. *"Him?"*

"Well, he speaks French," I said.

"That's not enough to make me want him, for God's sake. I mean, he wears aftershave!"

The second was a wrong move as well—way too finicky. "But he is good-looking," I said.

"What do I want with a good-looking boyfriend?" Hugh asked.

"Right," I said. "Thanks."

The latest one, though, a sheep farmer named Duncan—this time I'm really onto something. It's true that he's currently living with somebody, but at this point, so is Hugh. "There's no telling what might happen between now and when I die," I say. "Maybe Duncan's boyfriend will hit me with his car while driving drunk. I'll be killed instantly, he'll be sent to prison for manslaughter, and wham: the two of you are set."

I believe I'm being thoughtful, but Hugh doesn't see it that way. In fact, it infuriates him.

"Don't you want *me* to be happy after *you* die?" I ask.

"No," he says. "I want you to be alone and miserable. And if you *do* find someone, I'm going to return from the dead and haunt you."

This brings us back to ghosts, which, as I said, I don't believe in. I'm just too practical.

A Number of Reasons I've Been Depressed Lately

One. It's early September 2015 and I'm on the island of Santorini for a literary festival. After the short reading, which takes place outdoors on a patio, the Greek audience asks questions, the first of which is "What do you think of Donald Trump?"

Since announcing his candidacy, the reality-show star has been all over the news. Every outrageous thing he says is repeated and analyzed—like he's a real politician. I answer that I first became aware of Donald Trump in the late 1980s. That was when Alma, a Lithuanian woman I was working for, bought his book *The Art of the Deal* and decided that he was wonderful. Shortly afterward, I saw him on *Oprah*, and ever since then he's always been in the background, this ridiculous blowhard, part showman and part cartoon character. I see his presidential bid as just another commercial for himself. It wouldn't surprise me if he were to name the Hamburglar as his running mate. So I say that onstage and then have to explain who the Hamburglar is.

Two. A month before the election, a man picks me up at the Philadelphia airport and takes me to Red Bank, New Jersey, for a show. We get to talking and I learn that his name is Michael. He is white and fifty-five and used to work for Pathmark, a supermarket chain that went bankrupt and closed the last of its branches in 2015. I ask some general questions and learn that grocery stores make the bulk of their money on junk food. "The highest markup, though, is on spices—seventy-six percent!" Michael says, adding that the most frequently stolen items are razor blades, baby formula, and big jugs of laundry detergent, which seem like they'd be pretty hard to shoplift. I mean, those things have gotten huge, like gas cans.

"Nowadays people walk out with the whole cart," Michael says. "Roll out the door saying, 'Just try to stop me!'"

It's rare for a hired driver to overtly discuss politics, and rarer still for him or her to introduce the topic. They will sometimes skirt around it, though. We pass a trump sign on the road, and Michael acknowledges it, saying sourly, "I just feel that for guys like us, white guys our age, if we need any help—housing or food stamps or whatever—it's the back of the line. You know what I mean?"

Well, isn't that sort of where the line forms? I think. Michael is in a group I've been hearing a lot about lately. White men who, following eight years of a black president, feel forgotten.

How exactly did Obama neglect you? I want to ask but don't. Instead I change the subject to lines in general. "I didn't wait more than a few minutes to check in for my flight this morning," I say cheerfully, not adding that I'm Executive Platinum on American, so never have to wait for anything. When I do have to wait, I'm appalled.

Three. I donate a thousand dollars to the Hillary for President campaign, and within what seems like minutes I get an email from them saying, in effect, "That's great, but can we have more?" Her organization is by no means unique in this regard. Everyone I donate to acts the same way, and I wind up unsubscribing from their emails and resenting them.

Four. I talk to a longtime friend of the family, who tells me with great authority that Hillary Clinton is a member of the Illuminati and that she and her husband have killed scores of people, including children, whom they also sexually molested.

"You're kidding, right?" I say.

He's not, and within minutes words are shooting from his mouth like water from a fire hose. It's hard to catch them all, but I do grab hold of "You think it's a coincidence that Prince was murdered on Queen Elizabeth's birthday?"

"Who said that he was murdered?" I ask. "Oh please," this person says. "You honestly believe he died of an 'accidental drug overdose'?"

The guy speaks to me like I'm an idiot.

"And the queen had him killed ... why, exactly?" I ask. "Because his name was Prince?"

I later look at one of the websites this person relies upon for information. On it, an anonymous source close to the royal family—a "palace insider"—reports hearing the queen saying to another Illuminati member at a tea party that before the year ends three more world-famous musicians must die.

None of the websites my friend looks at say anything bad about Donald Trump. Rather, he is hailed as a man of peace. The ones they hate are George Soros, of course, and surprisingly Bill Gates, who has murdered more innocents than even the Clintons, apparently. My friend gets almost feverish when he talks about these people and the way they're all connected: Queen Elizabeth leads to Jay-Z leads to the Centers for Disease Control leads to the faked Sandy Hook shooting and the way the government staged 9/11.

I want to laugh. Then I want him to laugh and say, "Just kidding!" But he honestly believes all this and is frustrated that I won't believe it as well. "Wake up!" he says.

Five. An article in the *New York Times* suggests that Trump should run with the Hamburglar, and I think, *Hey, that's my line.*

*

Six. On election night I am in Portland, Oregon. At the start of the evening I feel confident, but come dinnertime I start to get nervous. I eat alone in the fancy hotel restaurant, watching the waiters and waitresses for clues that I am worrying over nothing. "Any news?" I keep asking, taking it for granted that, like me, they voted for Clinton. *They have ironic tattoos and know about wine. Who else could they have been for?* I think.

Back in the room I turn on the radio and look at the electoral map online. I go to bed, reach for my iPad. Shut my eyes, reach for my iPad. When the election is called for Trump, I lie there, unable to sleep. In the middle of the night I go to the fitness center and watch the little TV embedded in my elliptical machine. The news had been telling me for months that Clinton was a shoo-in. Now they want me to listen as they soul-search and determine how they got it so wrong. "Fuck you," I say to the little screen.

An hour later I take a bath and get back into bed. Staring at the ceiling, wide-awake, I suddenly think of Cher and realize that what I'm feeling, she's feeling as well. So are millions of other people, of course: Hugh, my sisters, all my friends except for the conspiracy theorist. Oddly, it's this woman I've never met or even seen in person who brings me comfort. The next morning I wander the city in a daze, my eyes bloodshot from lack of sleep, thinking, *I'm not alone. I've got Cher.*

Seven. A few days after the election I am in Oakland, California. It's Sunday afternoon and I notice a great many people walking toward what looks like a park, some of them carrying signs. "What's going on?" I ask a young woman. Her hair is purple in some places and green in others.

"Oh," she says, "everyone's going to Lake Merritt to hold hands. We're going to form a human chain around it." She says this as though it's going to reverse time and make Donald Trump stop being the president-elect. I cringe, thinking of how this will play on Fox News: "Watch out, everyone, they're holding hands!"

Eight. I join my family on Emerald Isle for Thanksgiving and have a great screaming fight with my Republican father, who yells at one point, "Donald Trump is *not* an asshole!" I find this funny but at the same time surprising. Regardless of whether you voted for him, I thought the president-elect's identity as a despicable human being was something we could all agree on. I mean, he pretty much *ran* on it.

Later in our argument my father shouts, "He's the best thing that's happened to this country in years!" and "It was just locker-room talk."

"I'm in locker rooms five days a week and have never heard anyone carry on like Trump in that video," I argue. "And if I *did,* I wouldn't think, *Wow, that guy ought to be my president.* I'd think he was a creep and a loser." Then I add, repeating something I'd heard from someone else, "Besides, he wasn't *in* a locker room; he was at work."

Since I left the United States in 1998, I've cast absentee ballots. Americans overseas vote from the last state they lived in, which for me was New York. Then we got the house on Emerald Isle and I changed my location to North Carolina, where I'm more inclined to feel hopeless. In 1996, in line at the grocery store in lower Manhattan, I'd look at the people in front of me, thinking, *Bill Clinton voter, Bill Clinton voter, convicted felon, Bill Clinton voter, foreign tourist, felon, felon, Bill Clinton voter, felon.*

At the Emerald Isle supermarket that I stomp off to after the fight with my father, it's *Trump, Trump, Trump, Trump, Trump,* and then the cashier, who also voted for him. Of course, these are just my assumptions. The guy in the T-shirt that pictures a semiautomatic rifle above the message COME AND TAKE IT, the one in fatigues buying two twelve-packs of beer and a tub of rice pudding, didn't necessarily vote Republican. He could have just stayed home on Election Day and force-fed the women he holds captive in the crawl space beneath his living room.

The morning after our argument, I come downstairs to find my father in the kitchen. "Are you still talking to me?" he asks. I look at him as if he were single-handedly responsible for the election of Donald Trump, as if he had knowingly cast the tiebreaking vote and all of what is to come is entirely his fault. Then I say, "Yes. Of course I'm still talking to you."

He turns and plods into the living room. "Horse's ass."

Nine. On Christmas morning, at home in England, I climb into the loft space above the bathroom in search of some presents I'd wrapped months earlier. The ladder I'm using is wooden and has only two legs, which slip on my freshly waxed floor. I fall from a height of nine feet and land with a bang on my left side, fracturing eight ribs. As I lie on the floor, stunned and in the greatest pain of my life, it occurs to me that I might die before Trump assumes office, and that maybe that won't be such a terrible thing. Amy runs out of the guest room then, and Hugh charges up the stairs from the kitchen, both of them asking, "What happened?" and "Are you all right?"

I don't want to ruin Christmas, so say, "I'm fine. I'm fine." Fine people, though, don't need ten minutes to get off the floor.

Hugh phones the NHS—the National Health Service—and after being asked a number of preliminary questions, I'm put through to a nurse named Mary.

"Who are you again?" I ask.

"Mary," she repeats, not, I notice, Mary Steward or whatever her last name is. Everything in America is based on law-suits, on establishing a trail. In the United States I'd be told to come in immediately for X-rays, but in England they figure that unless you're unconscious or leaking great quantities of fluid—blood, pus, etc.—there's no point in wasting everyone's time. Mary asks me a number of questions to determine whether I pierced a lung, which apparently I have not. "But it really hurts when I cough," I tell her.

"Well, David," she says brightly, "then my advice to you

would be not to cough, and to have a lovely Christmas."

I later learn that what I suffered was called blunt force trauma. It's remarkably similar to how I felt after the election, as if I'd been slammed against a wall or hit by a car. Both pains persist—show no signs, in fact, of ever going away. The damage is permanent. I will never be the same as I was before the accident/election. A lovely Christmas is out of the question. Every day I lie on the floor and clutch my sides, stunned.

Ten. I hold on to the most unreasonable hope. The electoral college will come to its senses and say, "We can't let this happen!" It will turn out that Russia tampered with our voting machines. Yet nothing stops the advancing truck. On Inauguration Day I am in Seattle. Late in the afternoon my old friend Lyn sends me a photo of an anti-Trump sticker someone found in Japan. It's cleverly designed: three peaks that on second glance turn out to be Trump sandwiched between two Klansmen. I want to write back and say Ha, but instead, as a joke, I respond, Dear Lyn, I'm sorry you're so opposed to change, or too small-minded to move past your narrow assumptions. In the future I'd appreciate your keeping things like this to yourself.—David

A minute later I send a follow-up email that says Just kidding. And it bounces back, as do the next three emails I send. *She's blocked me!* I realize. *After thirty-eight years of friendship!*

I go to bed that night and lie awake, worried that she's

telling everyone I'm a Trump supporter. The news will spread, and by morning I'll be ruined. "But it was just a joke," I say to myself in the dark room. "A horrible, horrible joke."

Why Aren't You Laughing?

From the outside, our house on the North Carolina coast—
the Sea Section—is nothing much to look at. It might have
been designed by a ten-year-old with a ruler, that's how
basic it is: walls, roof, windows, deck. It's easy to imagine
the architect putting down his crayon and shouting into the
next room, "I'm done. Can I watch TV now?"

Whenever I denigrate the place, Hugh reminds me that
it's the view that counts: the ocean we look out at. I see his
point, but it's not like you have to limit yourself to one or
the other. "What about West Sussex?" I say. From the outside our cottage in England resembles something you'd find
in a storybook—a home for potbellied trolls, benevolent
ones that smoke pipes. Built of stone in the late sixteenth

century, it has a pitched roof and little windows with panes the size of playing cards. We lie in bed and consider sheep grazing in the shadow of a verdant down. I especially love being there in winter, so it bothered me when I had to spend most of January and February working in the United States. Hugh came along, and toward the end we found ourselves on Maui, where I had a reading. I'd have been happy just to fly in and fly out, but Hugh likes to swim in the ocean, so we stayed for a week in a place he found online.

"Let me guess," the box-office manager of the theater I performed at said. "It's spread out over at least four levels and paneled in dark wood, like something you'd see on a 1970s TV show, right?"

He'd hit it squarely on the nose, especially the dark part. The wood on the interior walls had been rigorously stained and was almost the color of fudge, a stark contrast to the world outside, which was relentlessly, almost oppressively, bright. As for the various levels, any excuse seemed to have been taken to add stairs, even if only two or three. If you lived there full-time, you'd no doubt get the hang of them. As it was, I tripped or fell down at least twice a day. The house reminded me of the condominium units my family used to rent on Emerald Isle when I was in my twenties, though none of those had a crucifix hanging in the kitchen. This one was ten inches tall and supported a slender, miserable Christ plated in bronze.

That was the only decoration aside from a number of framed photo collages of the owner and his family taken over the years. They were a good-looking group, one that multiplied as the children grew and had kids of their own. The color in the earlier snapshots had faded, just as it has in pictures of my own family: same haircuts, same flared slacks and shirts with long droopy collars, only now drained of their vibrancy, like lawns in winter. Each generation looked healthy and prosperous, yet I found myself wondering what lurked beneath the surface—for surely there was something. "Which of you is in prison now?" I'd ask, glancing up as I tripped on the stairs to the bedroom.

The house was on the ocean, and the beach that began where the backyard ended was shaded with palms. Most often it was deserted, so except for a few short trips up the coast for supplies, Hugh stayed put during our week on Maui. If he wasn't on the deck overlooking the water, he was in the water looking back at the deck. He saw whales and sea turtles. He snorkeled. My only accomplishment was to sign my name to five thousand blank sheets of paper sent by my publisher. "Tip-ins," they're called. A month or two down the line, they'd be bound into copies of the book I had just about finished. There were still a few more weeks to make changes, but they could be only minor grammatical things. Hugh, who is good at spotting typos and used to do so for his father, a novelist, was reading the manuscript for the first time. Whenever I heard him laugh, I'd ask, "What's so funny?" Should five or ten minutes pass with no reaction, I'd call out, "Why aren't you laughing?"

*

It takes quite a while to sign your name five thousand times, so I set myself a daily goal and would stop whatever I was doing every two hours and pick up my Magic Marker. Often, while autographing, I'd listen to the radio or watch a TV show I like called *Intervention*. In it, real-life alcoholics and drug addicts are seen going about their business. Most are too far gone to hold down jobs, so mainly we see them starting fights, crying on unmade beds, and shooting up in hard-to-spot places like the valleys between their toes. Amazing, to me, is that anyone would allow him- or herself to be filmed in this condition. "Did you catch me on TV?" I'd imagine them saying to their friends. "Wasn't it incredible when I shit on that car?"

That's what a thirty-one-year-old drunk woman did in one of the episodes I watched as I signed blank sheets of paper: pulled down her pants, positioned herself just so, and defecated on the rear bumper of a parked Audi A4. As she went at it—a diamond shape blurring her from the waist down—I thought of my mother, in part because she was a lady. By this, I mean that she never wore pants, just skirts and dresses. She never left the house without makeup on and her hair styled. Whenever I see a young woman boarding a plane in her pajamas, or a guy in a T-shirt that reads your hole is my goal, I always wonder what Mom would think.

She's been dead almost thirty years, so she missed a lot of the buildup to what is now thought of as less-than-scandalous behavior. I once watched a show in which a group of young men were sent out to collect pubic hair. It was a contest of sorts, and in the end the loser had to put all the spoils on a pizza and eat it. That was in 2003, so, to me, someone on television shitting on a car—*Sure. OK. That makes sense.* To go there straight from *Murder, She Wrote*, however, would be quite a shock.

Another reason *Intervention* makes me think about my mother is that she was an alcoholic. It's a hard word to use for someone you love, and so my family avoided it. Rather, we'd whisper, among ourselves, that mom "had a problem," that she "could stand to cut back."

Sober, she was cheerful and charismatic, the kind of person who could—and would—talk to anyone. Unlike with our father, who makes jokes no one understands and leaves his listeners baffled and eager to get away, it was fun to hear what our mom might come out with. "I got them laughing" was a popular line in the stories she'd tell at the end of the day. The men who pumped her gas, the bank tellers, the receptionists at the dentist's office. "I got them laughing." Her specialty was the real-life story, perfected and condensed. These take work, and she'd go through a half dozen verbal drafts before getting one where she wanted it. Over the course of the day the line she *wished* she'd delivered in response to some question or comment—the zinger—would become the line she *had* delivered. "So I said to him, 'Buddy, that's why they invented the airplane.'"

We'd be on the sidelines, aghast: "That's not how it happened at all!" But what did it matter with such great results?

You'd think my mother could have seen the difference between the sunny, likable her and the dark one who'd call late at night. I could hear the ice cubes in her glass rushing forth whenever she took a sip. In my youth, when she'd join my father for a drink after work—"Just one, I have to get dinner on the table"—that was a happy sound. Now it was like a trigger being cocked.

"The little bitch," my mother would say, her voice slurred, referring to someone she might have spoken to that afternoon, or maybe five years earlier—a shop clerk, a neighbor. "Talking to *me* that way? Like *that?* Like I'm nothing? She doesn't know it, but I could buy and sell her."

Fly home for a visit, and you'd find her in the kitchen, slamming around, replaying some argument she'd had with our father. "Goddamn bastard, shove it up your ass, why don't you, you and your stinking 'Why hire a plumber when I can do it myself?' You *can't* do it yourself, you hear me, buddy? You *can't*." Late in her life, my mother embraced the word "fuck" but could never quite figure out its place in a sentence. "So I said to him, 'I don't give a damn fuck what you *do* with it, just get it the hell out of my driveway.'"

By that point in the evening she'd look different, raw, like you'd taken the lady she was earlier and peeled her. The loafers she favored would have been kicked off and she'd be in her stocking feet, hands on the counter to steady herself as she raged. She was hardly ever angry at the person she was talking to—exceptions being my brother, Paul; my father; and my sister Tiffany—rather, she'd be looking for support.

"Can you believe this shit? I mean, *can you?*" We didn't dare contradict her.

I have an English friend named Ingrid, and her father was an alcoholic. When he lost his license for driving drunk, he got himself a tricycle and would pedal it back and forth to a pub, everyone in the village watching.

"Not a regular bike?" I asked.

"He would have fallen off!" Ingrid told me, relieved to be at the stage where she could laugh about it. Her father was a horrible person, a mean clown, which makes it easier, in a way. Our mother did nothing so cartoonish, and if she had we'd have felt traitorous making fun of her. Instead, we separated her into two people and discounted what the second, drunk one did. For that wasn't really her, we reasoned, but a kind of virus talking. Her father had it too, and drank until men in white coats carted him off to the state hospital, where he received shock treatments. I look at pictures of him after his release and think, *Wait, that's me.* We didn't resemble each other when I was young, but now we could be twins.

The big moment on *Intervention* is when family and friends of the alcoholic or drug addict confront him or her. It's supervised by a counselor and often takes place in a sad hotel conference room with flesh-colored furniture and no windows. The addicts are usually in full blossom, drunk or high or on the nod. "What the hell ... ?" they say, looking around at their parents, their brothers and sisters, their wives or husbands, all together, seated in a semicircle.

The subjects of the intervention already feel ambushed, so steps are taken to keep them from feeling attacked as well. It's easy to lose one's temper in this situation, so the counselor has instructed the friends and family members to organize their thoughts on paper. The letters they read are never wholly negative and usually kick off with a pleasant memory. "I remember when you were brought home from the hospital" is a bigone. This is the equivalent of a short story beginning with the main character's alarm clock going off, and though I know I shouldn't get hung up on this part of the show, I do. *Oh please,* I think, rolling my eyes as the combative meth addict is told, "You had a smile that could light up a room."

The authors of the letters often cry, perhaps because what they've written is so poorly constructed. Then again, reality TV is fueled by tears. Take another of the shows I like, *My 600-lb Life,* about morbidly obese people struggling with their weight. At the start of each program loved ones appear, always weeping, always saying the exact same thing: "I don't want to have to bury my own child/sister/nephew, etc."

Yes, well, I wouldn't either, I think. If digging the grave didn't do me in, I'd surely die trying to roll that massive body into it. There's crying on *Hoarders* as well, though rarely by the pack rat, who sees no downside to saving all his used toilet paper.

After everyone on *Intervention* has had their say, the addicts are offered a spot in a rehab center. Not all of them accept, but most do. The places they're sent to tend to be sunny: Arizona, Southern California, Florida. We see them two months into their stay, most looking like completely different people. "Here are the wind chimes I made in my arts-and-crafts group," the woman who earlier in the program was seen shooting speed into her neck says.

Not everyone stays the prescribed ninety days. Some leave early and relapse. Others get out on schedule and relapse a week or six months later. The heartiest of them are revisited several years down the line, still sober, many with jobs now and children. "All that time I wasted," they say. "What on earth was I thinking?"

I asked Ingrid once if she ever talked to her father about his drinking, and I think she was ashamed to answer no. Not that I or anyone in my family ever confronted my mother, no matter how bad it got. Even my dad, who's superdirect and tells complete strangers that they're loud or wrong or too fat for that bolero jacket, said nothing. Then again, it built so gradually. For as long as I was living at home, it never seemed a problem. It was only after five of her six children had left that she upped her quota. The single Scotch before dinner became two, and then three. Her wine intake doubled. Tripled. She was never a quality drinker—quantity was what mattered. She bought jugs, not bottles. After dinner, she'd switch to coffee and then back to Scotch or wine, supplementing the alcohol with pills. "Mom's dolls," we called them.

When she told us that she would no longer drive at night, that she couldn't see the road, we all went along with it, knowing the real reason was that by sunset she was in no shape to get behind the wheel. "Gosh," we said, "we hope that doesn't happen to our eyes when we're your age."

In that respect, you have to hand it to the family members on *Intervention*. Corny letters notwithstanding, they have guts. The person they're confronting might storm out of the room and never talk to them again, but at least they're rolling the dice. Though we never called our mother on her behavior, she knew that we noticed it.

"I haven't had a drink in four days," she'd announce out of nowhere, usually over the phone. You could hear the struggle and the hope in her voice. I'd call her the next night and could tell right away that she'd lost her willpower. *Why aren't you stronger?* I wanted to ask. *I mean, really. Can't you just* try harder?

Of course, I was drunk too, so what could I say? I suppose I felt that my youth made it less sad. The vast plain of adulthood stretched before me, while she was well into her fifties, drinking alone in a house filled with crap. Even sober, she'd rail against that: all the junk my father dragged home and left in the yard or the basement—old newspapers and magazines, toaster ovens picked out of the trash, hoses, sheets of plywood—all of it "perfectly good," all of it just what he needed.

In my mind, our house used to be so merry. There was music playing in every room. The phone was always ringing.

People in my family laughed more than people in other families. I was as sure of that as I was of anything. Up and down the street, our neighbors left their dinner tables as soon as they could and beat it for the nearest TV. That's what my father did, while the rest of us stayed put with our mother, vying for her attention as the candles burned down. "Group therapy," she called it, though it was more like a master class. One of us would tell a story about our day and she'd interject every now and then to give notes. "You don't need all that detail about the bedroom," she'd say, or, "Maybe it's best to skip the part about the teacher and just cut to the chase."

"Pour me a cup of coffee," she'd say come ten o'clock, our empty plates still in front of us. "Get me another pack of Winstons from the pantry, will you?" One of the perks of having six kids was that you didn't have to locate anything on your own. "Find my car keys," she'd command, or, "Someone get me a pair of shoes."

There was never a rebellion, because it was *her* asking. Pleasing our mother was fun and easy and made us feel good.

"I'll light her cigarette ... "

"No, *I* will."

Maybe ours wasn't the house I'd have chosen had I been in charge of things. It wasn't as clean as I'd have liked. From the outside, it wasn't remarkable. We had no view, but still it was the place I held in mind, and proudly, when I thought, *Home*. It had been a living organism, but by the time I hit my late twenties it was rotting, a dead tooth in a row of seemingly healthy ones. When I was eleven, my father planted a line of olive bushes in front of the house. They were waist-high and formed a kind of fence. By the mid-eighties they were so overgrown that pedestrians had to quit the sidewalk and take to the street instead. People with trash to drop waited until they reached our yard to drop it, figuring the high grass would cover whatever beer can or plastic bag of dog shit they needed to discard. It was like the *Addams Family* house, which would have been fine had it still been merry, but it wasn't anymore. Our mother became the living ghost that haunted it, gaunt now and rattling ice cubes instead of chains.

I'd come home from Chicago, where I was living, and she would offer to throw a dinner party for my friends. "Invite the Seiglers," she'd say. "And, hey, Dean. Or Lyn. I haven't seen her for a while."

She was lonely for company, so I'd pick up the phone. By the time my guests arrived, she'd be wasted. My friends all noticed it—how could they not? Sitting at the table as she repeated a story for the third time—"I got them laughing"—watching as she stumbled, as the ash of her cigarette fell onto the floor, I'd cringe and then feel guilty for being embarrassed by her. Had I not once worn a top hat to meet her at the airport, a top hat *and* suspenders? With red platform shoes? I was seventeen that year, but still. And how many times had *I* been drunk or high at the table? Wasn't it maybe *my turn* to be the embarrassed one? *Must remain loyal,* I'd think.

The morning after a dinner party, her makeup applied but

still in her robe, my mother would be sheepish. "Well, it was nice to see Dean again." That would have been the perfect time to sit her down, to say, "Do you remember how out of control you were last night? What can we do to help you?" I'm forever thinking of all our missed opportunities—six kids and a husband, and not one of us spoke up. I imagine her at a rehab center in Arizona or California, a state she'd never been to. "Who knew I'd be so good at pottery?" I can hear her saying, and, "I'm really looking forward to rebuilding my life."

Sobriety would not have stopped the cancer that was quietly growing inside her, but it would have allowed her to hold her head up—to recall what it felt like to live without shame—if only for a few years.

"Do you think it was my fault that she drank?" my father asked not long ago. It's the assumption of an amateur, someone who stops after his second vodka tonic and quits taking his pain medication before the prescription runs out. It's almost laughable, this insistence on a reason. I think my mother was lonely without her children—her fan club. But I think she drank because she was an alcoholic.

"How can you watch that garbage?" Hugh would say whenever he walked into the house on Maui and caught me in front of *Intervention*.

"Well, I'm not *only* watching it," I'd tell him. "I'm also signing my name."

This was never enough for him. "You're in Hawaii, sitting

indoors in the middle of the day. Get out of here, why don't you? Get some sun."

And so I'd put on my shoes and take a walk, never on the beach but along the road, or through residential neighborhoods. I saw a good deal of trash—cans, bottles, fast-food wrappers—the same crap I see in England. I saw flattened cane toads with tire treads on them. I saw small birds with brilliant red heads. One afternoon, I pushed an SUV that had stalled in traffic. The driver was perhaps in his mid-twenties and was talking on the phone when I offered a hand. He nodded, so I took up my position at the rear and remembered after the first few yards what a complete pain in the ass it is to help someone in need. I thought he'd just steer to the curb, but instead he went another hundred or so feet down the road, where he turned the corner. "Does he expect me to ... push him ... all the way ... home?" I asked myself, panting.

Eventually he pulled over and put on the brake. The guy never thanked me, or even put down his phone. *Asshole*, I thought.

Back at the house, I took another stack of papers and started signing my name to them. "That's not your signature," Hugh said, frowning over my shoulder.

"It's what's *become* of my signature," I told him, looking at the scrawl in front of me. You could sort of make out a "D" and an "S," but the rest was like a silhouette of a mountain range, or a hospital patient's medical chart just before he's given the bad news. In my defense, it never occurred to me that I'd be signing my name five thousand times. In the course of my entire life, maybe, but not in one shot. This was not the adulthood that I had predicted for myself: an author of books, spending a week in Hawaii with his handsome, long-time boyfriend before deciding which house to return to. I had *wished* for it, sure, but I'd also wished for a complete head transplant.

Hugh had made himself a Manhattan and was sitting on the patio with my manuscript. A minute passed, then two. Then five. "Why aren't you laughing?" I called.

I was living in New York, still broke and unpublished, when my mother died. Aside from the occasional Sidney Sheldon novel, she wasn't a reader, so she didn't understand the world I was fluttering around the edges of. If she thought it was hopeless, or that I was wasting my time writing, she never said as much. My father,on the other hand, was more than happy to predict a dismal future. Perhaps it was to spite him that she supported us in our far-fetched endeavors—art school for me and Gretchen, Amy at Second City. Just when we needed money, at the moment before we had to ask for it, checks would arrive. "A little something to see you through," the accompanying notes would read. "Love, your old mother."

Was she sober in those moments? I wondered, signing my name to another sheet of paper. *Was it with a clear mind that she believed in us, or was it just the booze talking?*

The times I miss her most are when I see something she might have liked: a piece of jewelry or a painting. The view of a white sand beach off a balcony. Palm trees. How I'd have loved to spoil her with beautiful things. On one of her last birthdays I gave her a wasp's nest that I'd found in the woods. It was all I could afford—a nursery that bugs made and left behind. "I'll get you something better later," I promised.

"Of course you will," she said, reaching for her glass. "And whatever it is I'm sure I'm going to love it."

I'm Still Standing

In the spring of 2017 a passenger seated two rows ahead of me on a plane to Denver shit in his pants. He was old but not ancient—early eighties, maybe—and was traveling with a middle-aged woman I took to be his daughter.

"Oh *no*," I heard her moan.

The man responded with something I couldn't catch, and the woman, who was on her feet now, threw up her hands. "Well, I'd say it's a little more than an *accident*."

As the guy shuffled toward the bathroom, I lowered my eyes, the way I hope my fellow passengers will do when it's my turn to soil myself on a crowded airplane. For surely that day is coming. One late morning the person who's causing everyone to gag will be me. Teenagers will laugh, and as they raise their phones to take my picture from behind, their parents, to no avail, will scold them.

"The walk of shame," I call it. For it's not the first time I've seen someone slog from their now-ruined seat to the bathroom. A few years back, it was a woman, very nicely dressed, at least in my opinion. She looked like she'd taken her clothes off a long-dead Gypsy whose grave she had just now unearthed, and I smiled as she approached, thinking I would say to her, *What an interesting skirt*.

Then she drew closer and, well . . .

The man who'd shit in his pants went into the bathroom and stayed there, no doubt looking for something to kill himself with. When my turn comes I'm thinking I'll smash my glasses and open a vein with one of the shards. Because there's no coming back from a thing like that. It doesn't matter that you'll never see these people again. Even if the plane were to go down and everyone on it but you were to die instantly, you'd never really recover.

"Sir?" Fifteen minutes after the man entered the bathroom, one of the flight attendants began knocking on the door. "Sir, we're preparing to land. I'm afraid you need to come out and return to your seat." She knocked again. "Sir? Are you all right?"

For God's sake, leave him alone, I wanted to say. *It isn't fair to make him come out and walk past us all another time. Just let him be.*

Either the flight attendant came to her senses and stopped harassing him, or, after leaving the bathroom, the man took a seat in the back row. All I know is that I never saw him again. He was on my mind, though.

A few weeks after that flight, I was in Dallas, having lunch with my young friend Kimberly, when all of a sudden I didn't feel very well. It came out of nowhere, a nausea that caused me to lose my appetite and perspire, though I wasn't particularly hot. "I know of a place not far from here that serves the most amazing pie," Kimberly said after I successfully fought her for the check. "Are you up for a slice, maybe with ice cream?"

I didn't want to say that I wasn't feeling well. It ruins everyone's good time. *And besides,* I thought, *since when has pie made anything worse?*

Back at my hotel an hour or so later, I lay on my bed for a while, then raced to the bathroom. I didn't know where I'd gotten it from, but I seemed to have contracted a pretty serious gastrointestinal virus.

Unfortunately, I had a show to do. Two thousand people were expecting me to pull myself together, get dressed, and stand in front of them for an hour and a half. So that's what I did. It was the first time in my memory that I read while sitting down. The hope was that the pressure of my body might keep everything in that was threatening at any moment to gush out. By this point it was like rusty water, what seemed to be a paint can's worth every time. For ninety minutes all I thought of was how shitting my pants in front of that many people was going to feel. Not that it requires a great deal of imagination. It helped, I suppose, that I was behind a podium, and that the front row was a good twenty feet away, on the other side of the orchestra pit. The audience might never need to know. I'd have to kill the entire stage crew, though, including poor Kimberly, who was standing in the wings with a bucket in her hands—a bucket!—and was the only person I'd talked to about my condition.

One of the things I thought of that evening—for it is entirely possible to think of other things, and even to do math while reading out loud—was my friend Andy. A few months earlier he'd told me that when he was sixteen, and in his then-girlfriend's rec room with three of their fellow high school students, he started feeling queasy. "I think it was food poisoning from some stuffed shells I'd eaten," he said. "I was sweating, my stomach started churning, and just as I stood up to run to the bathroom, it poured out of me."

"Oh my God," I said. We were at his house eating dinner with his wife and two adolescent daughters, who had heard the story before but could clearly hear it again every day for the rest of their lives. I mean, their dad shitting in his pants—that's gold.

"I had to borrow clothes from my girlfriend's brother," Andy told us, his head in his hands, still haunted. "Not that he ever wanted them back. The relationship was over the moment I let loose on her family's carpet."

That's the kind of thing that would scar a person for life. It's, like, *Carrie* level.

"How are you not still in therapy?" I asked. "I mean, it's only been, what ... thirty years?"

Andy was in front of four other people, I thought, turning the page and looking up briefly from the podium. *Multiply that by five hundred.*

After the reading there was an equally precarious book signing. "Do you ever meet people who have a gastrointestinal virus?" I asked a woman after learning she was a nurse.

"Oh yes," she told me.

"And what do you recommend they do?"

"Well, there's not much you *can* do, really," she said. "Drink plenty of fluids, something with electrolytes like Gatorade. Rest. You probably don't feel like eating, but you should force yourself to get something down. That's all I can tell you."

I'd hoped that by the following morning I'd be back to normal, but there was no change. I'd gotten up three times during the night and was still passing a paint can's worth of rusty water every two hours or so. *Where on earth is this coming from?* I wondered. *My eyes? Did I have great stores of liquid hidden in my neck? My calves?* I had to go to Des Moines, so I put an extra pair of dark slacks in my carry-on tote bag, just in case the worst happened during the flight. I thought of picking up a ski mask as well—that's what you really need: something to conceal your identity as you make the walk of shame. But in this day and age—on a plane—a ski mask would only get you tackled. This while you're already nauseated and plastered with your own feces.

The thing about a stomach virus is that it exhausts you. Brushing my teeth wore me out. When it came time to put on my shoes, all I could do was stare down at them and whimper. At the airport I wanted nothing more than to rest. I couldn't, though, because I had my Fitbit to consider—that and the Apple Watch I wear right above it on the same wrist. Every night it sends me a notice congratulating me on my longest-running move streak. I'd met all my requirements— standing time, exercise minutes, and calories burned—for 360 days, and there was no way I was going to ruin my perfect record. The minimum for my Fitbit is four and a half miles, but for my watch it's closer to seven, hardly an unreasonable distance unless, like me, even standing upright is a challenge.

Yet still, after checking my suitcase, I put one foot in front of the other and dragged myself from Terminal A to D and back. "Must meet Fitbit and watch requirements," I moaned between clenched teeth, staggering forward. "Must be mentally *and* physically ill at the same time." Two miles later I boarded my flight and put what little energy I still had back into fearing I might shit in my pants in front of a planeful of people.

How is this my life? I asked myself as I settled into my seat with a bottle of Gatorade, perhaps the greatest indignity of all. "What flavor is that?" the man beside me asked.

I looked at the bottle. "Blue."

For that's all Gatorade ever tastes like—its color. Over the period that I had my stomach virus, I tried them all:

blue, red, green, yellow, orange, and a new opaque one that tasted opaque.

One of my watch's more irritating features is an hourly reminder to get off my ass. I'll often be at the podium toward the end of a show and feel what amounts to a light tap on my wrist, followed by a message: Time to stand up.

What do you think I've been doing for the past eighty minutes?

I want to shout, wondering where it gets its information from.

The watch is seemingly calibrated to whichever plane I'm on, so the moment we hit turbulence or are instructed to prepare for a landing, I can expect the tap. "Please sit down and fasten your seat belts," the flight attendant says.

Stand up and be my crazy slave, the watch counters.

I realized not long ago that if I put my hands in front of me and rub the palms together for a minute, the way I might if I were cold or were watching a very slow waiter bring something to my table that I was really looking forward to, I can fool the watch and be rewarded with the Congratulations, you did it! message.

Some would call this cheating, but on an average day I far exceed my standing goal, so in my mind I'm covered. Plus, I only rub my hands together when traveling. At home, when instructed to stand, I do something useful—empty the scrap bucket into the compost bin, hang a few shirts on the clothesline.

"Did you just do a load of laundry?" Hugh will ask.

"No," I'll tell him. "I just wanted to leave my desk and get a few steps in. Those shirts are dirty." At home I can adhere more strictly to my beloved routine, which has always been very important to me. More important than anything, I used to think. Then touring came along—aka money—and I decided I could maybe learn to wing it for a while.

In an average year I might spend three and a half months on the road, more if I have a new book out. "Does Hugh come with you?" people regularly ask.

"No," I tell them. "I mean, he'd like to, but what with his wheelchair it would be pretty hard."

The person who asked then nods respectfully, no doubt sorry that he or she brought it up.

"I have to wash him and feed him and get him in and out of bed. It takes a great deal of time, so when I'm away I hire someone to do all that for me."

Another understanding nod.

Sometimes I leave it at that, and sometimes I admit that I'm kidding and explain that Hugh has better things to do than accompany me to Des Moines. "I'm just surprised that you believed the wheelchair business," I say. "Not that there's anything wrong with being a quadriplegic, but given all the times I've mentioned Hugh in print, being paralyzed from the neck down is a pretty big thing to leave out, don't you think?"

*

At home, when I get sick or injured, Hugh will usually insist that it's all in my mind. Either that or he'll blame me for it. That was the case when I fell off a ladder. It was Christmas Day, and as I lay on the floor, unable to move or even speak, he stood over me shouting, "Why are you wearing those pants?" As if the legs were sewn together and were the reason I'd fallen. "You look like an idiot! And with that shirt I don't even know who you are anymore!"

Is now really the moment to get into all this? I wondered, fairly certain that my back was broken.

The time before that, though, he was so kind. This preceded the ladder incident, and also took place in Sussex. It was early December, and I was on my daily walk, perhaps seven miles from home, when I understood that something was wrong. My stomach didn't ache, exactly. Rather, it let its presence be known. Then I felt a sudden loss of energy, as if someone had reached inside me and yanked out my batteries.

The owner of the house I was in front of had placed large rocks on either side of his driveway and painted them white. The biggest was maybe six inches tall. It was uncomfortable to sit on, but I did, and a few moments later I vomited, grateful that it was almost dark and raining, and that no one could see me. Then I did it again, thinking this might be the only vomit in all of England that had no traces of alcohol in it—a novelty, but nevertheless unsightly. And so I covered it up with leaves before struggling to my feet.

Hugh's piano teacher lived a few houses away from the rock I'd been sitting on. It wasn't a great distance, but weak as I was, it took a while to reach her front door, then to form a fist and knock on it. Her husband kindly gave me a ride home, where I found Hugh in his studio, and vomited some more.

"Wow," he said. "You're really sick."

He helped me into the house and upstairs to our bed. Then he brought me a bell that I rang every ten or so minutes for the next sixteen hours. "Can I have some water?" "I think I need a glass of ginger ale. We don't have any? I bet the store does." "Bring me my iPad, my laptop, the memoir in my office by a man who had both his feet chewed off by a panda cub. You couldn't find such a book? Maybe I dreamed it. Where's that tea I asked for? Can you change my socks for me?"

I thought of Hugh quite often during the period that I had my stomach virus. He doesn't like to talk on the phone, and it's a mistake to push him on it. He'll settle for an email in a pinch, but what Hugh wants when I'm away are letters with stamps on them. If they're patched-together entries from my diary, he can tell and will stop reading. So I have to sit down with the express intent of addressing him and only him. I sometimes resent the time it takes, but then I picture him at home, taking the letter from Phil, our mailman, and laying it on the kitchen table. He won't read it right away. Rather, he'll prepare for it, sitting in the garden if it's dry, or in his studio if it's not. He'll have a cup of coffee or tea, and maybe a biscuit he's just whipped up: everything just so, the way I am if a *New Yorker* arrives with a story by Lorrie Moore in it.

Then I'll think of the way he eats dinner when I'm not there, of how he'll spoon the juices of whatever he prepared over the meat or fish, and arrange things attractively on his plate. When I'm alone, I'll sometimes eat directly out of the pans with my fingers to save myself from having to wash a fork or a dish, but not Hugh. He always sets the table before sitting down. If it's chilly he'll build a fire in the kitchen fireplace, and the flames will reflect off his wineglass. Then he'll light candles and eat with the same manners he'd use if invited to Buckingham Palace, a cloth napkin on his lap, not watching a show on his computer or reading anything but just staring forward, at the place where I would be if I were home. Whenever I get tired of having to write him letters, I think of that—him eating alone—and pick up my pen. "Dear Hugh ... "

While sick, I wrote that I wasn't feeling well. I said I worried I might shit in my pants on a plane or while standing at the podium, but even that was testing his limits. Unlike a friend of my brother's, who's been known to take pictures of his bowel movements and email them to his wife with the heading A puppy!!!, Hugh and I never discuss what goes on in the bathroom. I have no evidence he's ever done anything in there but brush his teeth and soak in the tub. He won't even let me in when he's peeing.

"I had that in my mouth ten minutes ago and now it's a private part?" I'll call from the other side of the door.

"Yes! Go away!"

If I'd had the gastrointestinal virus at home, I might have said, "I was in the bathroom a lot today." I could have spoken about my nausea and general lack of energy, but that would be the extent of it. I wouldn't use the word "diarrhea," as it would be too indelicate. We're well matched in our prudishness. The difference is that while I might not go into detail about *myself*, I'm more than happy to talk about someone else, this young man I met, for instance, whose girlfriend put her feet up on the dashboard of his truck and accidentally shit in her cutoff shorts. "I guess she got a little too relaxed," the guy told me.

"I don't want to hear this," Hugh said when I repeated the story.

We weren't eating or anything, but even if we were I wouldn't have understood his objection. "This happened years ago," I explained. "Thousands of miles away from here."

"That doesn't matter," he told me. "I'm not interested."

"But . . . "

"No."

My gastrointestinal virus lasted for six long days, each of which involved at least one flight and an appearance before an audience. Halfway through it, the cramps arrived, some so severe they doubled me over. I thought of my insides as a haunted house with bolts of lightning ricocheting off the walls. The worst of them came when I was in Austin, Texas, walking behind my hotel along a path that ran beside the river. I was trying to get my steps in, and as I stood there, legs crossed, my eyes screwed shut against the pain, it occurred to me that if the floodgates *did* open—which seemed highly probable—I'd have to jump into the water. Getting out again, wet, covered in mud, I'd likely wish I weren't staying in such a nice hotel. At the La Quinta Inn you might return to your room unnoticed, but there was no way I could sop through the lobby of the Four Seasons without causing a fuss. "A child was drowning, and I jumped into the river to save her," I could say. "Don't worry, she's fine now. I just need to go up and change out of these wet clothes."

Would they buy it? I wondered, looking out at the brown water. *Do I look like the type who could save a child? Should I add more detail—say, perhaps, that the girl was Mexican?*

These are the questions you ask yourself when you're traveling with a gastrointestinal virus. Then one day you wakeup normal, restored to health—a miracle. At first you're incredibly grateful—your appetite's back, and your energy level. There's a bit of you, though, that misses the razor's edge, the terrible thrill that at any moment you might lose control of yourself and finally know what total disgrace feels like. I'll wager that it's so far from *near* total disgrace as to be incomprehensible for a while. The difference, say, between a toothache and being burned alive. I think of that man in the airplane bathroom. The flight attendant knocks, thinking he has his trousers off and is trying to rinse them in that worthless little sink. But he's still fully dressed and looking in the mirror, shocked that he could feel so fundamentally different yet still have human features, let alone the same face. The two eyes right where they were the last time he checked, that same nose and mouth. *But how can this be?* he wonders.

"Sir," the woman on the other side of the door says. "Sir, you have to come out now. Sir? Are you all right?"

When it's my turn, I'll open my mouth, unable to speak, and feel a little tap on my wrist. Time to stand up, my watch will whisper.

Then, before killing myself, I'll say one last time, "I *am* standing up."

The Spirit World

Our house on Emerald Isle is divided down the middle and has an *E* beside one front door and a *W* beside the other. The east side is ruled by Hugh, and the bedroom we share is on the top floor. It opens onto a deck that overlooks the ocean and is next to Amy's room, which is the same size as ours but is shaped differently. Unlike Lisa and Paul, who are on the west side of the house and could probably sleep on burlap without noticing it, Amy likes nice sheets.

She'd packed a new set in her suitcase, and on the night before Thanksgiving, as I helped her make her bed, she mentioned a friend who'd come to her apartment for dinner the previous evening in New York. "He drinks Coke, right, so I went to the store on the corner to buy some," she said.

"And you know how those new bottles have names on the labels—Blake or Kelly or whatever?"

I nodded.

"Well, there were only two left on the shelf, one with Mom printed on it, and the other with Tiffany."

I reached for a pillowcase. "Do you think if I were dead there would have been three bottles on the shelf instead of two and the third would have had *my* name on it?"

Amy thought for a moment. "Yes."

"So the only Cokes at that store in New York City are for people in our family who have died?"

She smoothed out the bedspread. "Yes."

I couldn't tell if she honestly believed this. It's hard to say with Amy. On the one hand she's very pragmatic, and on the other she's open to just about anything. Astrology, for instance. I wouldn't call her a nut exactly, but she has paid good money to have her chart done, and if you're talking about someone, she'll often ask when this person's birthday is and then say something like "Ah, a Gemini. OK. That makes sense now."

She's big on acupuncture as well, which I also tend to think is dubious, at least for things like allergies. That said, I admire people who are curious and open their minds to new possibilities, especially after a certain age. You have to draw the line somewhere, though, and with me it's my anus. When I was in my early thirties, it became a thing to have colonics. A number of my friends started going to a man in Chicago and discussing the rubble he'd discovered in their lower intestines. "A pumpkin seed, and I haven't eaten pump-kin in eight years!"

Their insides were like pharaohs' tombs, dark catacombs littered with ancient relics. Now people are giving themselves coffee enemas, believing it wards off and even cures cancer.

"I think I'll take the cancer, thank you," my sister Lisa said to me on Thanksgiving morning.

"Amen to that," I agreed.

Lisa's not open to the things that Paul and Amy are, but she has her equivalents. If you told her, for instance, that she was holding her car keys the wrong way and that there were meetings for people like her, she'd likely attend them for at least three months. One of the groups she was going to lately was for mindful eating. "It's not about dieting—we don't believe in that," she said. "You're supposed to carry on as usual: three meals a day, plus snacks and desserts or whatever. The difference is that now you *think* about it." She then confessed that the doughnut she'd just finished had been her sixth of the day. "Who *brought* these?" she asked.

I looked at the box and whimpered a little. "Kathy, I think."

"Goddamn her," Lisa whispered.

A few weeks before we came to the beach, Amy paid a great deal of money to visit a well-known psychic. The woman has a long waiting list, but somebody pulled a few strings, and, not long after getting the idea, Amy had her session, which took place over the phone and lasted for an hour. She sent me a brief email after it was over and went into greater detail as we rode with Gretchen from the Raleigh airport to Emerald Isle the day before Thanksgiving. "So start again from the top," I said. "Was it scary?"

"It was maybe like calling someone in prison and having one person after another get on the line," she said from the backseat. "First I talked to Mom for a while, who's doing well, by the way, and takes credit for setting up you and Hugh. Then Tiffany appeared."

I ripped open a bag of almonds. "Yeah, right."

"Ordinarily I'd be like that too," Amy said, "but the psychic's voice changed after Mom went away. She sounded tough all of a sudden and started by saying, 'I really don't feel like talking to you right now. This is a *favor*, OK?'"

Tiffany thanked Amy for cleaning up the mess she'd left after she'd committed suicide.

"That's strange," I said. "I mean, how would the psychic have known anything about that?"

Amy sat up and moved closer, so that her head was between my seat and Gretchen's. "I know! She said that Tiffany had tried to kill herself before—also true—and that she always knew that she was going to do this, the only question was when. It was crazy how much she got right. 'Your sister was mentally ill,' she said. 'Possibly bipolar, and stopped taking her medication because she didn't want to dull herself.' She said Tiffany felt like everyone was taking from her, using her."

"That was certainly true," I said.

"Most of what Tiffany had to say was directed at you,"

Amy told me. "She wants you to know that the two of you are OK now, that she's not mad anymore."

"*She's* not mad!" I said. "*Her? I'm* the one who had reason to be mad."

"She said she'd misunderstood you and that lately she's been working on herself."

"You have to work on yourself *after* you're dead?" I asked. It seemed a bit much, like having to continue a diet or your participation in AA. I thought that death let you off the hook when it came to certain things, that it somehow purified you.

"Tiffany's been hanging out a lot with Mom's dad, Grandpa Leonard," Amy told me.

This made me furious for some reason. "But she didn't even *know* him."

"I guess they met there," Amy said. "And where is that?"

Amy shrugged. "I don't know. It's not like you can ask a thousand questions and get them answered. They tell you what they want to tell you and you just listen."

I tried to let that sink in.

"She and Mom are finally getting along," Amy continued. "She mainly wanted to let you know that she has no hard feelings. The psychic said Tiffany's been trying to tell you this herself and asked if you've had a lot of problems with your phone lately."

"No."

"Power outages?" Again I said no.

"What about butterflies?"

"Are you serious?" I asked. "Our house last winter was

231

loaded with them. I've never seen anything like it. In the summer, fine, but this was crazy. Hugh and I talked about it every day."

Amy crossed her arms. "It was Tiffany. She was trying to contact you."

The appointment with the psychic had unnerved the whole family. "Tiffany was calmer than normal, but still it was like an actual conversation with her," Amy said. "You remember how those were, right? We'd be shaking while they were going on. Then we'd think about them for weeks afterward."

"I remember," Gretchen and I said at the same time.

After Tiffany signed off, Amy spoke to an actor she'd known who died of a heroin overdose a few years back, and to her first serious boyfriend, John Tsokantis, who had a brain aneurysm when he was twenty-five.

Because she'd had a session so recently, I was welcome to cut to the front of the line and have one of my own the following week. "Do you want me to give you the psychic's number?"

I said nothing.

"Is that a no?" Amy asked.

Often, when signing books, I'll pretend to have powers. "Well, look at the Scorpio," I'll say when someone approaches my table. I'm just guessing—I wouldn't know a Scorpio from a double Sagittarius. The key, I learned, is to speak with authority. It's never "Are you a Libra?" but, rather, "It's about time I had a Libra up in here."

Every now and then I'll be right, and the person will be shocked. "How did you know my sign?" they'll ask.

"The same way I know you have a sister."

If I'm right about the sister as well, the person I'm talking to will become like a cat released into a new setting, very low to the ground and suspicious. "Who were you talking to? Did one of my friends put you up to this?"

I met a young woman a few years back, and after being right about both her sign *and* her sister, I said, as if I were trying to recall something I had dreamed, "You were in a . . . hospital earlier this week, not for yourself but for someone else. You were . . . visiting someone very close to you."

The woman fell apart before my eyes. "My mother has cancer. They operated but . . . How do you . . . I don't . . . What are you doing?"

"I can't help it," I told her. "I know things. I see them."

I don't, of course. Those were just guesses, pulled out of my ass in order to get a rise out of someone.

Hugh said the psychic Amy went to did the same thing, but I'm not sure. "How would she know what Tiffany sounded like?"

"Looked her up on YouTube," he said. "Read one of your stories. These people tell you what you want to hear. It's their way of getting you to come back."

There's something about picking the psychic apart that I don't like. It's cynical and uninteresting. That said, I knew I didn't want to book a session. My mother and I were very close, and though I miss her terribly, I'm not sure I need to talk to her again. Since her death I'd thought of it as an impossibility. Now it felt like a decision, like Mom wants to speak to me and I'm saying no. But what if she's angry at me for some reason? What would I do with that?

As for Tiffany, a few months after she died, a Dutch film crew came to Sussex and followed me around for three days. Our conversation was all over the place—we talked about England, writing, life with Hugh. The last hour was shot on a hilltop overlooking my house. The interviewer, a man named Wim, sat beside me. Off camera he'd mentioned that my sister had recently taken her life. Now he brought it up again. "What if you could ask her one question?"

It seemed like such a television moment, the intimacy unearned—grotesque, almost. And so I paused and blinked hard. Then I said, "I'd ask ... 'Can I have back that money I loaned you?'"

What troubled me most about Amy's talk with the psychic was the notion that the dead are unsettled. That they linger. I said to Lisa at the beach that Thanksgiving, "If they can see us from wherever they are, what's to stop them from watching us on the toilet?" Lisa took a moment to consider this. "I'm guessing that certain places are just ... off-limits."

"And who would make them off-limits?" I asked.

"I don't know," she said. "God, maybe. I mean ... beats me."

We were returning from a walk and came upon our father in the middle of the street a quarter mile from the house. He was dressed in jeans and had a flat-topped cap on his head. His flannel shirt was untucked, and the tail of it drooped from beneath the hem of his Windbreaker. "What are you doing here?" I asked.

"Looking for someone," he said.

Lisa asked who, and he said he didn't know. "I was just hoping somebody might come along and invite me to his house to watch the game. The Panthers are playing this afternoon, and you don't have a goddamn TV."

"You thought someone was just going to say, 'Hey, why don't you come to my place and watch some football?'" Lisa asked.

"I was going to build up to it," my father said. "You know, drop hints and so forth."

The day after Thanksgiving was bright and unseasonably warm. Hugh made ham sandwiches for lunch and we ate on the deck. "We need to have a code word so when the next one of us dies, we'll know if the psychic is for real," Amy said. She turned to Dad, the most likely candidate for ceasing to live. "What'll yours be?"

He gave it no thought. "Ecstasy."

"Like the drug?" I asked.

He picked up his sandwich. "What drug?"

"It should be something you say a lot," I told him. "Something that would let us know it's really you. Maybe . . . 'You've gained weight' or 'Obama's from Kenya.'"

"Those are both three words," Lisa noted.

235

"What about 'Broderson'?" I said, referring to a North Carolina painter whose work my father collected in the 1970s.

"Oh, that's perfect," Amy said.

I went into the kitchen to get another napkin, and by the time I returned, the topic had changed and Dad was discussing someone who goes to his gym. The guy is in his forties and apparently stands too close in the locker room. "He undresses me with his eyes, and it makes me uncomfortable," my father said.

"How does someone undress you with his eyes when you're already undressed?" I asked. "By that point what's he looking at, your soul?"

On our final evening at the beach over the Thanksgiving weekend, Amy and my niece, Madelyn, usually host a spa night. They dress in uniforms and let it be known beforehand that clients are expected to tip, and generously. Facials are given, and Kathy offers foot massages. The treatments feel great, but the best part is listening to Amy, who plays the role of the supervisor. This year, while massaging clay onto my father's face, she asked him if he was alone this evening or with his gay lover. "I know that a lot of men such as yourself also like their testicles waxed," Amy said. "If that is of any interest to you, sir, I can get my trainee, Madelyn, right on it. Maddy, you up for this?"

It's so subversive, not just insisting that our father is gay but that his twelve-year-old granddaughter might want to rip the hair off his balls.

Before the clay is rubbed into our faces, we're outfitted in shower caps, and afterward, while it dries, we lie back with cucumber slices on our eyes. Paul programs his iPad to play spa music, or what passes for music in such places, the sound of a waterfall or rustling leaves. A whale saying something nice to another whale. A harp. This year I lifted the cucumbers off my eyes and saw Lisa and Dad stretched out like corpses, fast asleep. Paul was out as well, and Gretchen, whose legs were shin-deep in the warm whirling bath, was getting there.

It seems there was a perfectly good explanation for all the butterflies in our Sussex house the previous winter. From what I'd read since Amy brought it up, they flew in through our windows in early autumn, then passed into a kind of hibernation. Hugh and I were away until right before Christmas, and when we returned and cranked up the heat, the butterflies, mainly tortoiseshells—dozens and dozens of them—awoke, wrongly believing that spring had arrived. They were on all the second-floor windows, batting against the panes, desperate to get out.

As symbols go, they're a bit too sweet, right for Lisa but all wrong for Tiffany, who'd have been better represented by something more dynamic—crows, maybe. Two big ones flew down the chimney of my office that winter and tore the place apart, systematically overturning and then shitting on everything I cared about.

What, I wondered, placing the cucumbers back over my eyes, *would my symbol be?*

The last time I saw my sister Tiffany was at the stage door at Symphony Hall in Boston. I'd just finished a show and was getting ready to sign books when I heard her say, "David. David, it's me."

We hadn't spoken in four years at that point, and I was shocked by her appearance. Tiffany always looked like my mother when she was young. Now she looked like my mother when she was old, though at the time she couldn't have been more than forty-five. "It's me, Tiffany." She held up a paper bag with the Starbucks logo on it. Her shoes looked like she'd found them in a trash can. "I have something for you."

There was a security guard holding the stage door open, and I said to him, "Will you close that, please?" I had filled the house that night. I was in charge—Mr. Sedaris. "The door," I repeated. "I'd like for you to close it now."

And so the man did. He shut the door in my sister's face, and I never saw her or spoke to her again. Not when she was evicted from her apartment. Not when she was raped. Not when she was hospitalized after her first suicide attempt. She was, I told myself, someone else's problem. I couldn't deal with her anymore.

"Well," the rest of my family said, "it was Tiffany. Don't be too hard on yourself. We all know how she can be."

Perhaps, like the psychic, they were just telling me what I needed to hear, something to ease my conscience and make me feel that underneath it all I'm no different from anyone else. They've always done that for me, my family. It's what keeps me coming back.

And While You're Up There, Check On My Prostate

The summer after I turned sixteen, I took driver's ed from a coach at my high school and quickly realized that this was not for me. Turning invoked a great deal of anxiety, as did staying in my lane, and parking—oh, parking—that was the worst. I suppose I could have tried harder to overcome my fear and discomfort, but I didn't, and as a result I have never gotten a ticket, made a car payment, or called anyone a fucking piece of shit asshole through an open or closed driver's-side window. It's not that I never get angry, just that I never get angry the way people behind a wheel do. My fury isn't poetry, just greeting-card prose: "Go to hell, you."

"What do you say when someone cuts you off in traffic?" I asked a woman in Copenhagen whose book I was signing.

"We're not big on cursing," she told me, "so the worst we're likely to come out with—and it's pretty common—is 'Why don't you run around in my ass?'"

There are asses in America where that might not be much of a threat. This is to say that, though it would be dark in there, and it probably wouldn't smell so great, at least you'd have some room to spread out. It would be more like a prison cell than, say, a coffin.

I'd asked the same question a few years earlier in Amsterdam and learned that in the Netherlands you're more apt to bring a disease into it. "Like if someone drives in a crazy way, it's normal to call them a cholera sufferer," a Dutch woman told me. "Either that or a cancer whore."

I'd never thought of stitching those two particular words together. "A *cancer whore?*" I asked.

She nodded. "I'm pretty sure it comes from The Hague."

The following day I checked out her story with a woman named Els, who said, "Oh, sure. Cancer whore. I hear it all the time. You can also say 'cancer slut.'" She added that the words are pretty much the same in Dutch as they are in English. "We say '*slet*,'" she said. "*Kanker slet.*"

"Would you ever call someone a ... I don't know ... a *diabetes slet?*" I asked.

She looked at me as if I were missing out on something so fundamental, it was a wonder I could dress myself in the morning. "Of course not," she said. "The disease has to be terminal."

"So, like, AIDS whore?"

Again she seemed exasperated. "AIDS? Never. Those poor people—that's not funny! If you want to be creative you say something like 'dirty typhus Mongoloid,' which you hear a lot lately." She paused. "Is that the right word, 'Mongoloid'?"

"We would say, 'person with Down syndrome,'" I told her. "But I guess that when joined with the words 'dirty' and 'typhus,' it would be too long. Especially when you're passing someone on the highway."

They're strange, the Dutch. After talking to Els, I met a man who frequently calls his eighteen-month-old daughter a "little ball sack." "Because, I mean, it's what you do," he explained.

"What do you mean 'it's what you do'?" I said. "It's not what *I* do or anyone in my family does. I don't even call my ball sack a ball sack."

He shrugged, Dutchily.

In Vienna, I returned to my original question: "What do Austrians yell out their car windows when they get angry?"

"Well," a young woman told me, "sometimes we will say, 'Why don't you find a spot on my ass that you would like to lick and lick it?'"

I'm guessing this is quicker to say and less awkward-sounding in German. Even so, it lacks a certain something. "You give them a choice of where to lick your ass?" I asked. "That doesn't sound like much of a threat, given that they could pick a spot on the side or up top, where it's basically just your lower back."

She agreed. "And sometimes if the bad driver is a female, we will call her a blood sausage."

"Is that because a woman has a period?" I asked.

"Maybe."

Later that night I met a Bulgarian. "In my country, you say to someone you hate, 'May you build a house from your kidney stones.'"

Well, finally, I thought. This is essentially wishing someone an eternity of gut-wrenching pain, all for taking the parking space you wanted or not turning his blinker on. I've had three kidney stones in my life, each the size of a small piece of gravel you might find at the bottom of an aquarium, and each excruciating. The thought of passing enough of them to build an entire house—even if it was just big enough for a termite to live in—is unfathomable. Those Bulgarians don't fool around, though no one can come close to the Romanians.

At a book signing in Boston, I met a woman from Bucharest. "My publicist is Romanian," I told her. "Not full-blooded like you, but still she can speak a little. Her favorite saying, taught to her by her grandmother, is 'I shit in ... ' God, what is that? ... 'I shit in ... ' "

"'I shit in your mother's mouth'?" she asked. "That's probably what it was. It's a very popular curse."

The woman walked away, and I thought, *Well, I can see why.* "I shit in your mother's mouth." Does it get any nastier than that?

I discovered a year later on my first trip to Bucharest that, actually, yes, it does. "What's the absolute worst thing you've ever heard?" I asked from the stage at the end of my reading. People lined up with answers, and I learned that, as in all Catholic and Eastern Orthodox countries, the most popular target when on the attack is the other person's mother. Thus: "I fuck your mother's dead, I fuck your mother's Christ, I fuck your mother's icon, I fuck your mother's Easter, I fuck your mother's onion, I will make skis out of your mother's cross," and "I fuck your mother's memorial cake." This is something you bake when a loved one dies, and there's a lot of cursing centered around it, the absolute worst being "I dragged my balls across your mother's memorial cake, from cherry to cherry, and to each of the candles."

A young woman told me this, and when I repeated it to the fellow who drove me to the airport the following morning and who had previously been chatty, he fell silent.

"That is total devastation," he eventually said. "I mean, wow. What kind of a person told you this? Was it a girl? Was she pretty?"

The Romanians really do lead the world when it comes to cursing. "What have you got for me?" I asked a woman from Transylvania who was now living in Vienna.

"Shove your hand up my ass and jerk off my shit," she offered.

I was stunned. "Anyone else would say, 'Shove your hand up my ass,' and then run out of imagination," I told her. "You people, though, you just keep going. And that's what makes you the champions you are."

243

Maybe it's not too late to learn how to drive, I thought, watching as she walked out the door and onto the unsuspecting streets of Vienna, this poet, this queen, this glittering jewel in a city of flint.

The Comey Memo

It was mid-August on Emerald Isle, and so far no one had drowned or been attacked by sharks. This was good news for the local Realtors, one of whom, a cheerful woman named Phyllis, had become a family friend. Hugh dropped by to see her the day after we arrived and returned an hour or so later with a flushed face.

"Guess who's staying twelve houses down? James Comey, that's who! He came into the office earlier this week and had his picture taken with Sherry."

I went out to the deck, where Gretchen was hanging up her wet swimsuit. "You'll never believe who's staying eight houses away. Jim Comey." She pulled a clothespin out of her mouth. "Wow, you're kidding!"

245

Next I told my niece, Madelyn, who is fourteen. She looked up dully from her phone and said, "Who?"

The woman behind the counter at the post office responded the same way.

"You know," I told her. "The guy who's all over the news lately?"

"Oh my God," she said. "How long has he been here?"

I had no idea but didn't want to sound like I was out of the loop. "Five days. And he's only a few houses away from me!"

I could practically hear the phone being dialed as I left. "Guess who's on the 7400 block of Ocean Drive?"

"You *what?*" Hugh said when I told him I'd told the postmistress. "Now *everyone* will know!"

I wrote my friend Lynette and was about to write our neighbor Lee when I found Hugh writing him. "It's *my* news, not yours," he hissed.

Late that afternoon we rented a golf cart. The girls took it out just before sunset and turned around in James Comey's driveway. "At least I think it was his," my sister-in-law, Kathy, reported at dinner that night. "There was a black SUV with Virginia plates and dark windows parked out front."

After eating we all jumped into the golf cart and drove by the house twice. "Look, lights are on!"

Rental units turned over at noon the following day, so we never got a chance to see him, this former director of the FBI whom we all hated until someone we hated even more fired him.

"Oh well," Amy said. "It was fun to be excited for a while. Now we can all go back to doing nothing."

Aside from Jim Comey, the big topic that week was our father, who was supposed to join us but had to cancel when his ride fell through. He'd lost his license earlier in the summer, and we'd all heaved a collective sigh of relief. Now we learned that he'd returned to the DMV with a letter from his eye doctor and gotten it back. "I followed him home from a dental appointment last week and couldn't believe it," Kathy said late one evening, lighting a cigarette on the deck that overlooks the ocean. "He has double vision and was all over the road. It's a miracle he didn't hit someone."

My father lives on his Social Security. He won't touch his savings or investments, which are substantial, as he wants to leave as much as possible to his children. It's what kept him alive during the Obama years, the hope that whoever succeeded him would eliminate the estate tax. It would be the perfect irony, then, for him to get into an accident and lose everything in a lawsuit. Lisa's fear is that he'll kill a child. None of the rest of us have gotten that specific, though I suppose she has a point. Killing a toddler sounds a lot worse than killing a fellow ninety-four-year-old.

"I'm getting regular calls from the neighbors now," Amy told me. "So are Paul and Lisa. 'Y'all need to be doing more for your father,' they say. 'He's too old to be living in that big house all on his own.'"

I thought of the last time I'd visited him, two years earlier.

Hugh and I were driving from Emerald Isle to the Raleigh airport and thought we'd drop in before flying back to England. I phoned again and again to say we were coming and left any number of messages. He hadn't responded, though, and because of his age, I started to wonder if maybe he was dead. On the three-hour ride to his house, I considered how probable this actually was. "Why don't you go in first?" I said to Hugh when we got to the house.

"Hello?" he called, sticking his head in the door. I stood behind him and looked through the window to see my father scuttling around the corner. "Hey, now, this is a surprise!"

I followed Hugh into the kitchen. "I left five or six messages," I said, relieved by how relieved I felt.

I'm guessing he'd set his air conditioner on ninety-eight—two degrees cooler than it was outside—which I didn't even know was possible. The heat and stillness made everything I saw look worse. My father's stove stopped working years ago, so he used his microwave to boil water and make us cups of instant coffee. We stood by the refrigerator, sweating. Then he asked if Hugh would advise him on a painting he had. "It's just here, around the corner," he said, grabbing a flashlight and stepping into what used to be a hallway but now had a chair and a table loaded with papers in it.

"Is the overhead light out?" I asked. "Want me to change it?"

"No, it's fine," my father said.

"So you use the flashlight ... ?"

"To save electricity," he explained.

We saw the painting my father was referring to the way a burglar might, the beam roving from spot to spot before sliding to the floor.

"If he won't move, why won't he at least get a housekeeper to come in once a week?" Hugh asked after we'd left and were on our way to the airport, me so depressed I was finding it hard to breathe. "Better yet, he could hire someone to live with him."

"That person might rip him off," I whispered. "Why are you whispering?" Hugh asked.

"So the people in the next car won't know there's a broken stove at my father's house they can steal."

Even if conditions hadn't grown worse over the past two years, my father would need to make some sort of change. "What I can't understand," I said to Amy on the beach one afternoon, "is *not wanting* to move! Who *wouldn't* prefer a new environment, a clean slate? He can afford to keep his house exactly as it is—could pay someone to drive him over every day and wait outside while he stacks up junk mail."

"You're trying to convince *me?*" Amy asked. "The one who has a second apartment two blocks from her first apartment just so she can get away from her rabbit for a couple of hours a day?"

According to Kathy, Lisa took my father to look at two different retirement communities not far from his house in Raleigh. "*Not* nursing homes," my sister assured him. "There are people as young as sixty-five living here."

"Your dad said he liked the first place, but when an apartment opened up he claimed he couldn't possibly move until he fixes up the house he's living in."

"He's been saying that for *fifty years,*" I told her.

Amy reached for her water bottle. "Dad refuses to move, and when I tell his neighbors that, they say, 'Well, then, you need to *make* him.' They're all thinking we don't care, but how do you *make* Dad do something?"

"Part of the problem," I explained to Hugh, who was stretched out beside me with a floppy hat over his face, "is that our father hates old people—always has. If everyone else in the retirement home was twenty, he'd be a lot more likely to give it a try, especially if they were all girls and all they were allowed to wear were bikini bottoms." I rubbed some sunblock onto my reddening forehead. "I can't believe we missed James Comey."

Two days later, Amy, Hugh, and I headed to Raleigh, the plan being to drop by my dad's place before continuing on to the airport. At a Starbucks a few miles from his house, we picked up four cups of coffee. I was holding one for myself and another for my father when we walked through his front door. "We're here!"

He wasn't in the kitchen, so after pausing to note the pair of briefs balled up and lying on my mother's beloved butcher-block table, we moved down the hall and looked into bedrooms I hadn't seen in years. Each was in the same state. His first step is to move in a table he can use as a desk. This will eventually be piled so high with papers that the stacks will topple onto the floor or, likelier still, into boxes that sit on the floor and have even more papers in them. The beds will have towering stacks upon them as well, and the various mounds will continue to grow until he crowds himself out and moves on to the next bedroom. There are five of them, including his own, which is at the end of the hall.

"Dad?"

Ten years earlier, my father, Amy, and I attended a wedding in Florida and stayed at a hotel in Delray Beach. "How did you sleep?" I asked over breakfast the next morning.

He thought for a moment. "I slept like a doll."

Perhaps he meant "I slept like a baby" and it came out wrong, but ever since, it's what everyone in my family says: "I slept like a doll."

My father so loved his bed at the hotel that Amy and I bought him one, explaining that what made it nice wasn't just the mattress but the sheets, which were high quality and, more important still, clean. The bed my father slept on in Florida would have vomited its stuffing had it seen its filthy twin in North Carolina. There was a narrow space for a person to lie on, but the rest of it, like the rest of the room itself, was piled high with bank statements, along with catalogs and belts and pages torn from newspapers. It was hard to pick out any one thing—rather, it blurred into a continuous mass, sort of like a glacier.

Overlooking it all, balanced atop a stack of twenty-year-old golf magazines on his highboy, were a half dozen photos of the family taken on Emerald Isle in 1981 and arranged under glass in a single frame. In them, Lisa looks amazing. All us kids do. It was that moment in a family's life when everything is golden, literally. Our tans were phenomenal, but so was our outlook. Ranging in age from twelve to twenty-four, my brother, sisters, and I gazed into the future and saw only promise.

It's not like we *don't* see it now. We're not pessimists, exactly, but in late middle age, when you envision your life ten years down the line, you're more likely to see a bedpan than a Tony Award. That our younger, cuter, infinitely more hopeful selves oversaw such total chaos made it all the sadder. I was just wondering what the house would look like had my mother been the surviving parent when I noticed my father on the deck just off his bedroom, staring into a tree. I'd last seen him a month earlier and had noticed how hunched over he was—not bent into the shape of a question mark, the way some people his age are, but still it made him look frailer. "Hey!" he said as I opened the sliding glass door. "There you are!"

He wore white tennis shorts with a beige T-shirt and matching socks. Everything looked too big on him: his watch, his glasses, even his teeth—which is odd, as they're completely his own. When he stepped forward to hug me, I noticed four mean-looking bruises on his arm. They weren't purple but black, and had cotton balls over them held down with masking tape.

"We brought you a cup of coffee," I said.

"Fantastic!"

The living room is the last semi-presentable patch of territory in my father's house—the only one without a desk in it—so we retired there. "Gosh, you all look terrific," he said, taking a seat on the sofa. "So tanned and healthy."

"What happened to your arm?" I asked.

"I fell," he told me, waving away my concern. "It happens sometimes when I turn around too quickly."

"So you fall, and then what?"

"I crawl around for a while until I come to a chair or something, and then I lift myself up.

"Hey," he said to Amy, no doubt eager to change the subject, "I pulled out a few things I thought you might like." He gestured to a pile on a low table beside the sofa. "There's a straw hat that belonged to your mother and some pocket-books."

"I don't really wear hats," Amy told him.

I didn't want my father to feel bad, so I picked it up. "The only bit that really says 'woman' is the bow," I said, walking into the bathroom to try it on and noticing that both the sinks were filled with stuffed animals. It was like they had planned to take a bath and were just waiting for someone to turn the water on. *What on earth?* I thought. "I can't believe that the straw's still in such good shape," I called into the other room.

"Isn't it?" my father called back.

"I've got a little something for you too," he said as I

reclaimed my seat, the hat still on my head. "Just a few things I knew you'd like."

On top of my pile were two Brueghel postcards. Both were in inexpensive plastic frames, bought that way, I assumed.

"He's someone you like, right?"

"Yes," I said. "Thank you so much."

Beneath the postcards were a couple of nature calendars, the first of which had a fox on the cover, nuzzling her kit.

"Isn't that terrific! I thought maybe you'd want to frame it."

"Hmmmm," I said. My father has criticized every gift I've ever given him. His disapproval is consistently swift and hard, but for some reason I can never respond in kind. "How nice," I told him.

The second calendar was devoted to chimps. "I know how much you like them. And these photos, I'm telling you, they're just outstanding."

I opened it to March and saw an adult male with his arms crossed, not defiantly but as if he were trying to make up his mind about something: whether to rip off the photographer's hands or to start with his face, most likely. Then I noticed that the calendar was two years old. "Well," I announced, looking at my watch, "I guess we'd better get going."

Amy and I were too shaken up to say much of anything in the car—underpants on Mom's butcher-block table!—so we just looked out the windows until we reached the airport.

There we learned there was "weather" in Washington, DC, where Hugh and I were headed.

"Well, where *isn't* there weather?" I whined, looking up at the board. "Can't they be more specific?"

Amy's flight to New York had been affected by distant storms as well. It was one of those times when your flights are delayed, and then delayed again. The DC departure time moved from seven to eight, then eventually to nine forty-five. Amy's flight was canceled altogether, so she wound up catching a taxi and spending the night in a hotel. After sitting around for a while, Hugh and I decided we might as well eat dinner. There weren't many choices at that hour, so we went to the 42nd St. Oyster Bar.

"This is where my mom and dad were the night Martin Luther King was assassinated," I said to Hugh after we had ordered. "Not here at the airport, obviously, but at their original location downtown." I told him how someone had stepped out of the kitchen to announce the news, and how everyone but my parents had applauded. "Our family hadn't been in the South very long, and that was a real eye-opener."

"Hmmm," Hugh said, pulling out his phone. "I'm just going to text Amy and see if she was able to book a flight for tomorrow morning."

I looked around at our fellow diners, all on their way to somewhere else, but all I could think about was my father, crawling through his house in search of a chair he could use to hoist himself up. He'd said it so matter-of-factly, "What I do . . . ," as if I'd asked how he makes a sandwich.

There are any number of people who have to live like that when they get to be terribly old, but for him it's a choice. My father could have a nice place. There could be help at the ready should he fall: a cook, a driver, someone to make the bed every morning. He's just too cheap to pay for it. "The killer," I said to Hugh, who had finished texting Amy and was now texting someone else, "is that he's saving the money to give to his kids, who will spend it wildly without even thinking. Maybe not Lisa, but you've seen everyone else in action. A person could live handsomely on the money we waste over the course of a given year, and here's our father wandering from room to room with a flashlight. He falls and gets banged up, then covers his bruises with cotton balls and masking tape because *Band-Aids* are too expensive!"

"Why don't you pay to get him a driver?" Hugh asked.

"Because he can afford it on his own," I told him.

Of course, Hugh was right—I should at least offer to pay. Like anyone else, my father loves free stuff. I was hesitating, in part, because he'd cut me out of his will.

"You told me you wanted to be cut out," he'd said five years earlier when I confronted him about it.

"When?" I asked.

"I don't know, but you did."

There was no way on earth that this was true. In that respect my father is very much like the current president: *There were a million and a half people at my inauguration. The biggest crowd ever—a million and a half!*

It's hard to even call it lying; rather, it's a form of insistence. *This is the way I need it to be, goddamn it.*

He then told me I could pick something out of the house and he'd set it aside for me to inherit. I looked around at the furniture, all of it covered with papers, and at the gloomy artwork he and my mother had bought in the seventies. "There's a guide for mixing drinks you have downstairs behind the bar," I said. "A bawdy paperback from 1960 illustrated by a cartoonist named Vip. I wouldn't mind having that, I suppose."

"But you don't even drink," he said.

I sighed. "You know what? You're right. It's better you give it to Amy, or Paul. One of them might want a Pink Squirrel some night."

Our food was delivered, and I said to Hugh, "I don't remember ever fighting with my mom, but with me and my dad it was constant. Once, in high school, he was shouting at me for something or other—running too much bathwater, maybe—and I shouted back, 'You are going to die alone!' Isn't that awful?" I pushed some shrimp and grits around my plate. "Now here he is, trying to do just that—die alone— and everyone's giving him a hard time about it."

When our check came, I paid. Hugh went to our gate, but there was still an hour to kill before boarding, so I took a walk from one end of the terminal to the other, then back again, passing the now shuttered Brooks Brothers, the Starbucks, the bookstore. This terminal didn't exist when

I lived in Chicago or New York. The Raleigh airport was smaller and slower back then. I'd fly home for a visit and wait at the baggage claim for half an hour before calling the house.

My father would answer—a bad sign, as it was he who was supposed to pick me up. "Did you forget I was flying in?" I'd ask. "I told you my plane was landing at six."

"Well, it's not six yet."

"Dad, it's six thirty."

"No, it's not."

"I'm looking at the clock in the airport and at my watch, and both say six thirty."

"Well, it's sure as hell not six thirty here, but I'm on my way. I'm leaving the house right now."

Twenty minutes later I'd phone again, and again he would pick up. I could hear his TV in the background. "I told you I'm on my way. Jesus!"

I'd wish then that I could afford to go to the ticket counter and buy a seat on the next plane back to where I'd come from. My father would arrive to pick me up, and I'd be gone, a speck in the sky.

"The secret to Dad's longevity isn't diet or exercise, or even his genes," I've often said to Paul and my sisters. "He's just late for death, the way he's been late for everything else all his life."

There are things I avoid talking about with my father now— politics, for instance. He's always operated on the assumption that I don't know anything, can't know anything, really. The issues are as far beyond my grasp as they are for the chimps in the calendar he gave me. Sure, one might pull a lever in a voting booth, but there could be no actual thought behind it.

The fight we had following Trump's election had been particularly ugly, and we could easily have it again every hour of every day. I don't want to, though, don't want what could be the last words we say to each other to be ugly. It's why I didn't bring up Jim Comey during our visit. Easier to put on a straw hat that once belonged to my mother and to accept with grace the framed postcards and nature calendars I dropped into an airport trash can before boarding my flight to Washington. It wasn't where they belonged, necessarily. It was just where they ended up.